THE BUSINESS WORLD
VOLUME ONE

CHAPTER ONE:
THE BEGINNING

Getting into the entertainment business; or even any business; hard to get into, and by getting the contacts you need; is something a person needs to find; the information; so in this book; it seemed that the information is there.

COMPANIES TO CONTACT ARE:

ITunes Licensing

1-800-793-9378

B-Smooth Production:

Inezbeson

1-773220-7700

1423 E. 68th St.

Ste. C

Chicago, IL 60637

Non-exclusive deal

Boost Digital Independent Music

P. O. Box 578

Crows Nest NWS

1585

Australia

61-2-9959-4405

Boost Digital Group Pty Limited

Level 6

220 Pacific Highway

Crows Nest

NSW

2065

Australia

Shalestone10@yahoo.com

Auctionsongs.com

Audiostreet.com

Banduniverse.com

Broadjams.com

Davidbowie.com

Clearchannerlnewmusic.com

Cornerband.com

Cstream.com

Dmusic.com

Faircopy.cm

Freshnewmedia.com

Funender.com

Hightidemusic.com

Hiptingle.spydigital.com

Howdoisound.com

Independentartistscompany.com

Indiconestop.com

Indiepad.com

Indiepodcasting.com

Itsaboutmusic.com

Itsfun.com

Jukeboxalive.com

Musicgrants.com

Musicmatch.com

Myorignalmusic.com

Musicspawn.com

Netmusic.com

Liquidaudio.com

Audiocandy.com

Digibag.com

Digitalsoundboard.net

Disclogic.com

Downlaadmusicmart.com

Listentoartistdirect.com

Justenoughtv.com

Listenup247.com

Localtracks.com

Mediakinesis.com

Mixposure.com

Modarchive.com

Mp3alliance.com

Mp3unsigned.com

Mperia.com

Musicforte.com

Musicgorilla.com

Themusictap.com

Musiciannetwork.com

Muzik101.com

Myjonesmusic.com

Newmusic-showcase.com

Gail Martin=1-410-290-5638

Isound.com/mp3s/gailmarten_and_the_chem_ehoff.trio/

Blam-Cee Edwards CEO

Xtremadness Entertainment LLC

SICA Soundz Publishing

10 E. Soulz Publishing

Avenel, NJ 07001

1-732-713-6383

Kings Garden Publishing/Rainbow Children Publishing/Jeremiah Semien Publishing

274 Highland Rd.

Ville Platte, LA 70586

Or other address:

123 Gobert Rd.

Ville Platte, LA 70856

New Power Network Records/King Of Music Records

Kings Garden Records/New Generation Records

Kings Garden Enterprise/New Generation Enterprise

Jerry Records/Jerry International Records/Jeremiah Semien Records

Queen Records

274 Highland Rd.

Ville Platte, LA 70586

Or

123 Gobert Rd.

Ville Platte, LA 70586

Alliances of Artists & Recording Companies

700 N. Fairfax St.

Alexandria, VA 22314

1-703-535-8101

Fax: 1-703-535-8105

Email: contact@aarcroyalties.com

Sound Wrekz Entertainment

812 Mars St.

Destin, FL 32541

Degy Management Services Inc.

Attention: Justin

6 Industrial Way W.

Ste. C

Eaton, NJ 07724

1-732-544-8000

1-732-544-5600

Broadcasting Music Incorporation (Performance Rights Organization) [New York Office]

320 West 57th Street

New York, NY 10019

1-212-586-2000

Facsimile: 1-212-245-8986

Red House Records

Ellen Stanley

P. O. Box 4044

St. Paul, MN 55104

Budge Tapes

Attention: John

3708 Macorkle Ave.

S. E.

Charleston, WV 25304

rlapse@releaserecords.com

Digital Distribution:

Buzzplay.com

Cannibalmusic.com

Decentxposure.com

Catchmusic.net

Music4ipods.com

Musicsceneonline.com

Msuictorch.com

Phonector.com

Worldphonic.com

New York Office

BMI (Broadcast Music)

320 West 57th Street

New York, NY 10019

212-586-2000

Fax: 1-212-245-8986

Electronic Mail Address: newyork@bmi.com

Los Angeles Office

8730 Sunset Boulevard

Third Floor

Los Angeles, CA 90069

1-310-659-9109

Fax: 1-310-657-6947

Electronic Mail Address: losangeles@bmi.com

Nashville Office

10 Music Square East

Nashville, TN 37203

1-615-401-2000

Fax: 1-615-401-2707

Electronic Mail Address: nashville@bmi.com

Miami Office

5201 Blue Lagoon Drive

Suite 310

Miami, FL 33126

1-305-266-3636

Fax: 1-305-266-2442

Electronic Mail Address: miami@bmi.com

London Office

79 Harley House

Marylebonne Road

London NW1 5HN

England

011-44-207-486-2036

Fax: 011-44-207-224-1046

Electronic Mail Address:London@bmi.com

Internet:

http://www.bmi.com

The Glossary

Published by the songwriters guild foundation

The Songwriters Guild of America

1500 Harbor Blvd.

Weehawken, NJ 07087

1-201-867-7603

National Music Publishers Association Inc./Harry Fox Agency Inc.

711 Third Avenue

New York, NY 10017

1-212-370-5330

Music Publishing

A Songwriter's Guide

Writer's Digest Books

1507 Dana Avenue

Cincinnati, OH 45207

ASCAP (American Society of Composers, Authors and Publishers) Offices:

New York:

One Lincoln Plaza

New York, NY 10023

Administrative: 1-212-621-6000

Membership: 1-212-621-6240

Fax: 1-212-724-9064

Los Angeles:

7920 W.Sunset Blvd.

3rd Floor

Los Angeles, CA 90046

1-323-883-1000

Fax; 1-323-883-1049

Nashville:

Two Square West

Nashville, TN 37203

1-615-742-5000

Fax: 1-615-742-5020

Atlanta:

PMB 400

541 Tenth Street

NW

Atlanta, GA 30318-5713

1-404-351-1224

Fax: 1-404-351-1252

Chicago:

1608 N. Milwaukee

Suite 1007

Chicago, IL 60647

1-773-394-4286

Fax: 1-773-3945639

Miami:

420 Lincoln Road

Suite 385

Miami Beach, FL 33139

1-305-673-3446

Fax: 1-305-673-2446

London:

8 Cork Street

London WIX 1PB

011-44-207-439-0909

Fax: 011-44-207-434-0073

Puerto Rico:

654 Ave. Munoz Rivera

IBM Plaza Ste. 1101 B

Hato Rey, Puerto Rico 00918

1-787-281-0782

Fax: 1-787-767-2805

Also call for membership: 1-800-95-ASCAP, or 1-212-621-6016

Electronic Mail Address: info@ascap.com

Internet:

http://www.ascap.com

SESAC (Society of European Songwriters, Authors and Composers)

Nashville:

55 Music Square East

Nashville, TN 37203

1-615-320-0055

Fax: 1-615-321-6290

Los Angeles:

501 Santa Monica Blvd.

Suite 450

Santa Monica, CA 90401-2430

1-310-393-9671

Fax: 1-310-393-6497

New York:

152 West 57th Floor

New York, NY 10019

1-212-586-3450

Fax: 1-212-489-5699

London:

6 Kenrick Place

London W1H 3FF

020-7486-9994

Fax: 020-7486-9929

www.sesac.com

CHAPTER TWO: THE NEXT STEP

The Film deals are a risky business; just as getting a job.

Anyone can go online; search for different films online.

Credits; could be at the beginning of the film; it could be at the end; of the film:

Executive Producer: Kings Garden/New Generation/King Of Music Enterprise/New Generation Films

Co-Producer: J-Man Pictures and Jeremiah Semien Films

Assistant Producer: Jerry Hollywood

Producers: J. J. and J, Michael

Directors: J-Roc and Lil Jerry

Co-Directors: Jerry Doggy Dogg and Randy

Assistant Director: J-Wood

Supervisor Of Photography: King Semien

Music By: Disc Jockey Jerry

Writers: Eric and Edmond

Chief Editors: Jereme and J

Photographers: Bubba and Mayo

Story Credit: Jeremiah Semien

Camera Operator: King Jerry

Assistant To Jerry: Jerry J.

Music Editor: Brother Jereme

Music Supervisors: Bradley and Joe

Casting Directors: J. J. Rhymes and Jerry Jones

Production Designers: John Myer and Barret

Composers: Boo and Boo-Boo

Cinematographers: J. R. and Jethro

Grips: Kevin and Isaiah

Gaffers: Jerome and J. S.

Foley: Parrain

Swing Gangs: S. B. and Bouncer

Best Boy: Daddy Jerry

Boom Man: Bigg Baller

Colour Time: Chief

Grip: Jeremiah Bradley Dies Semien Guillory

Key Grip: J-Man

Matte Painter: The Symbol Man

Soundtrack Supervisor: Prince

Promoters: Bigg Daddy Jerry and Bad Boy Jerry

Music Publishers: Kings Garden Publisher-BMI, Rain Bow Children Publisher-ASCAP, and Jeremiah Semien Publisher-SESAC

Publicist: Bigg Boy Jerry

Film Coordinator: Son

Singers: J. J. and the Zydeco New Breeze, and J. J. and the Zydeco New Breed

Record Labels: Kings Garden Records, New Generation Records, Jerry International Records, Jerry Records, Jeremiah Semien Records, New Power Network Records, Queen Records, King Of Music Records

Magazine Publisher: J-Man Publishing

Book Publisher: New Generation Publishing

Clothing Line: Jerry Wear

Wardrobe Coordinator: Uncle Jeremiah

Screen Play (Script) Supervisors: Uncle Jerry and Uncle G.

Senior System Administrator: Road Runner

Head Of Production: Jeremiah Castile

Editorial Coordinators: Emeril and Ricky

Production Accountant: Jean Pierre

Assistant Camera Operator: Jerry Dangerous

Assistant Video Editor: Easy Money

Architects: J. Paul, Chef Paul Prudhomme, Doctor Phillip McGraw (Doctor Phil), Jerold G., Mitch, Jerold, Sister Sledge. Papa, Jeremiah Johnson, Lightning, Jeremiah Derange, Line Cook, J-Boy, Moe, Abendnego, K. O., Daniel and Big Boy

Research Team: R. A. A., King Of Hollywood, Cow Boy, Jerry Jam, Jer Ray, Larry, Curly, Boss, and Shane

Okay; some contact information's are:

infotsubmissions@ticklebooth.com

Links to the videos, your name, and why I like it

Submit films: shortfilms@badamitr.com

Submit films; which are:

Pay Attention

C/o CPW

59 Tinker St.

Woodstock, NY 12498

Phone: 1-845-679-9957

Email: aeiel@cpw.org

Send tape, and Artist resume

Knitting Factory

Video Lounge

P. O. Box 1220

Canal St. Station, NY 10013

Send tape, short biography, and a self address stamp envelope

911 Media Arts Center

117 Yale Ave. N.

Seattle, WA 98109

Phone: 10296-682-6552

Email: peter@911media.org

Send tape, and Resume

Orgone Cinema and Archive

2238 Murray Ave.

Pittsburg, PA 15217

Send tapes

CHAPTER THREE:
THE CHANCE OF A LIFETIME

Trying your hand; in writing scripts; is not bad; at all:

Sylvia-Amy Lynn Dashavoo

Canada-Prince George- B C

Gunslinger Production

Horror scripts, no vampires, werewolves, and zombies

Carmichael Film

Drama/thriller

Gay script such as: Brother 2 brother, 24th Day, Last Good-Bye, and Unknown Solider

PTN Films P/L

Fantasy/Science Fiction scripts

Fantastic/ Futuristic or Unreal World

Futuristic-earthly world

Dark gothic fantasy world

Vulnerability of humanity

And human psyche

Such films like:

The crow, the matrix, and the lord of the rings

24th day-a married man; who picks up gay guys, but one of them have aids

Fax only: attention: development-vortex pictures

Query first/query letter

Christine Media

Email: Christine@screenmedia.net

Pandora=1-818-333-5023

4000 Warner Boulevard

Building 148

Suite 200

Burbank, CA 91522

Odyseey Entertainment

1 Berkeley Street

London, United Kingdom

W 1 8BJ

44-207-016-8847

Moon Stone

Horror Only

P. O. Box 7400

Studio City, CA 91614

1-818-985-3003

Fax: 1-818-985-3009

Kings Garden Enterprise/New Generation Enterprise/J-Man Pictures/King Of Music Enterprise/Jeremiah Semien Films/New Generation Films

274 Highland Rd.

Ville Platte, LA 70586

Or

123 Gobert Rd.

Ville Platte, LA 70586

Keller Entertainment Group

1422 Ventura Boulevard

Sherman Oaks, CA 91423

1-818-981-4950

Fax: 1-818-501-6224

D. J. Donnelly Productions Group Ltd.

P G D G TV

P.O Box 250

12455 South Powerline Road

Pompano Beach, FL 33069

1-347733-2913

Liversa Film

7974 Mission Bonita Drive

San Diego, CA 92120

1-619-286-8383

Fax: 1-619-286-8324

Email: Karl.Kozak@home.com

Attention: Aranon Orgers

Curb Entertainment

Email: curbfilm@earthlink.net

Fax: 1-310-553-9895 for Crystal Sky

Corey Marr Productions Incs

Email: info@coreymarr.com

Celestial Picture

Shaw Administration

Building

Lot 220

Clearwater Bay Road

Kowloon, Hong Kong852-2927-1111

1-848-333-5203

Fax: attention: Zack Cecchi Gori Group

13 Capella International Inc.

9242 Beverly Boulevard

Suite 280

Beverly Hills, CA 90210-3710

1-310-247-4700

1-310-247-4701

Email: scoot@artistviewent.co

Arch Light Pictures

1201/39 McLain Street

North Sydney

2060 Australia

61-2-9955-8825

Amesell Entertainment

12001 Ventura Place

Suite 404

Studio City, CA 91604

1-818-766-8500

Fax: 1-818-766-7873

Horror email: steven@americanworldpictures.com

1-818-380-9100

Allied Entertainment Group

8899 Beverly Blvd.

Ste. 911

West Hollywood, CA 90048

1-310-271-0703

Fax: 1-310-271-0706

Email: teddy_U2@hotmail.com-email for contact information

Rob Davidson

P.O. Box 230

Braidwood

NSW

2622

Australia

Attention: Vicki Watson

Music Director

Allegheny Mountain Radio

Route 1 Box 139

Dunmore, WV 24134

Cranial Explosions

P. O. Box 22177

Regina, Saskatchewan

Canada

S4S 7H4

Include a biography

For more information:

distributors@logoedcd.com

Email: standaloneproductions@hotmail.com

kellypubproduction@yahoo.com

stlandry@ilovegoodnews.com

sead@shadango.com

Educational scripts/ 20-30 minutes/pages:

tim@topfivefilms.org

Teen issues driven/date abuse/suicide/rape/etc

sailawaywithme66@yahoo.com

New poker & gambling movie

Pays $25-$75 length and quality

Shadango

Stand Media Inc

The Century Tower

20th Floor

Ste. 2007

Avendia Ricardo J. Alfaro

Panama City

Republic of Panama

604-608-5674

This company seeking screenplay writers:

seaviewmotionpictures@juno.com

Screenplay writers required:

everyone@everyonewhosanyone.com

Theresa Peoples/Cannell Studios:

tpeoples@cannell.com

Looking for a script;

networkfilms@gmail.com

Seeking Script:

15 pages; fiction/non-fiction; small cast; short list of character:

info@transformativefilm.com

Looking for complete; dark edge & supernatural/Horror Films:

Rafael@americanworldpictures.com

Send sample chapters/Seeking Writers:

Timdrake812@hotmail.com

Drama/action/adventure/me tap mystical/spiritual/fantasy/sci-fi

Based in south Florida/Caribbean-all must be comedy

joel@ide-tv.com

Need good writer:

mikepriest@mobilevideoproductions.com

Looking for finish script:

Effenskatevid@hotmail.com

Looking for complete horror scripts:

erin@level1.com

Looking for two types of complete; screenplays:

gavin@rampage-entertainment.com

Seeking writer for hire to Pen horror script/send resume:

cherea@media-blasters.com

Senior Marketing Writer:

Publications@mail.barry.edu

Seek Writers/send resume:

Film7070@msn.com

frogproudctions@europe.com

New Writers:

adampierson@99yahoo.com

Scripts have to be: 80-95 pages

Genre: supernatural/psychological horror script

No white house's; grocery stores interior; weather; elements; exterior snow; rain; wind; no articulated mechanical monsters; car chases; mass extended shots of mass destruction

300 words, or less summary

jeff@highervaluemovies.com

Romance & Comedies; as well as: horror/vampire scripts; fire fighters stories; strong erotically elements

Gruenberg@gruenbergfilm.de

10 minute short/drama

info@rockfallfilms.co.uk

5 minutes/3 characters

storymaker_syndicate@yahoo.co.uk

Ambiguous/healthily metaphorical/metaphysical themes

se_ade@shadango.com

Renegade Theatre Company:

Reading series; plays should be socially relevant, or deal w/teenage/adult issues

The dream factory

Comedy writers wanted: send pictures

Resume & brief description of what comedy is; email: thedreamfactory@aol.com

Duncan/YMCA

Staged reading series; mail play

Reality Show:

Reality show; concept wanted; bio & concept

realityshowpilot@yahoo.com

The artistic home:

Short plays & scenes; 20 pages/minutes, or less w/small cast

GPO

Gay theme

performingartsproductions@hotmail.com

10 page/minutes; 20 page/minutes; make sure under 45 page/minutes

bailwick.org

View Plays Wanted:

Contact Michael Pieper-1-773-772-7583

Spiritual/inspirational synopsis:

15 pages

info@transformativefilms.com

Estate Write for permission

Dark98502@aol.com

Science set in Russia; Latin America/central America; Middle East; Caribbean

Hispanic market-soap opera

ebsla@ebsla.com

Contact info; summary; horror/creature

Query letter; resume; bio

info@artmill.org

Send log line; synopsis; send sample writings; the 1st-5 pages

Island scripts:

hawaiiqueries@ninjagoldfish.com

Summary; contact info; horror:

hourglassfilms@shaw.ca

Thriller; mystery; strong character driver; comedy; memorable characters w/compelling hook

pdaula355@cs.com

www.spryfilms.com

postmasters@spryfilms.com

Advance instructions of submissions policy:

kokopelli-films@cox.net

Query:

claritypictures.net

submissions@claritypictures.com

hardssixprodutions.com

They will pay $5,000 for screenplay

Broger01@yahoo.com

Only family movies

Family/Comedy Movies

kellyspubprodictions@yahoo.com

linlea.com

Drama Love Story

cubeprod@globeliness.com.ph

Horror Movies/Scripts

Attention: Monster

Have to be 100 pages

james@paradisefx.com

Drama/Romantic/Comedy/Thriller/Horror

Short/Long Scripts

orfilms@gmail.com
Resume/Writing Samples

Attention: Development

producers@merlionfilms.com

New Branch Theatre Company

Scripts

Christian Themes & musicals

Submissions

C/O: Marvel Enterprise Inc.

10 E. 40th St.

New York, NY 10016

Writers; inquire letter; details of your writing experience; why would you like to write for Marvel Comics

Fan Light Productions

Attention: Acquisitions

Cargo

Scripts; films & documentaries

Cargoreleasing.com

Cinema Guild

Documentaries & fiction

Cinema Libre

Documentaries; provocative

Cinemalibrestudios.com

Direct Cinema

Short dramatic & animated films

Directcinema.com

Empire

Documentaries

Empirepictures.com

Film DVD

Unusual documentaries, or extreme horror & independent (indie) dramas

Filmthreatdvd.com

Frame line

Lesbian; Gay; Bi-sexual; Transgender (LGBT) queer films

Any genre

Frameline.org

Indican

Inventive; niche films

Indicanpictures.com

7th Art

Documentaries

7thart.com

TLA Releasing

Any films/gay films

Tlareleasing.com

Wolfe Video

Lesbian; Gay; Bi-sexual; Transgender (LGBT) content

Wolfevideo.com

Zeitgeist

Documentaries

CHAPTER FOUR:
WELCOME TO THE ENTERTAINMENT BUSINESS

Example of a short screen play/script:

PORNOGRAPHICAL BODIES

Fade In:

Scene I:

This scene takes place in, sunny, Palm Springs, California.

In this scene Kevin Johnson is in the precinct.

Ricky Martin:

Kevin, I wanted to know, if you were coming to patrol with me.

Kevin Johnson:

Yeah, let me finish with this paper work.

Ricky Martin:

Okay, I'll be in the car.

A soon as Kevin Johnson was finish, with his paper work; he went outside, to find Ricky.

Ricky was in the third, police vehicle, waiting for Kevin Johnson.

Kevin Johnson:

I am ready, let's go.

Ricky Martin:

Alright

Brother.

As they started riding, Ricky starts talking to Kevin Johnson.

Ricky Martin:

Kevin, I wanted to know, if you and I, are going to hook-up, tonight.

Kevin Johnson:

Yeah, brother, if you want to.

We are supposed to be, solving the case, that, the chief assigned us.

Ricky Martin:

We will, just after, a little rendezvous, between, you and I.

So, Ricky starts pulling in, his driveway.

Then, Kevin and Ricky gets out and enter Ricky's house.

Then, they start kissing, and next, they start, taking their clothes, off.

A few minutes, later, the two of them, get dress, and they walk outside.

Suddenly, the communicator goes off, in the patrol car and the dispatcher says:

Dispatcher:

If any patrol cars, in the area, there is a mystery man, which has broke into, James Madison's house.

If anyone picks up, you can go to his house, and get a statement.

Ricky Martin picks up.

Ricky Martin:

This is Ricky.

I am headed for James' house right now.

So, Ricky Martin and Kevin Johnson, rushed into the vehicle, and headed to James Madison's house.

As soon, as they had gotten there, they were greeted, by Officer John McNeil.

John McNeil:

Kevin, I want you, to see something.

Kevin Johnson:

Okay.

So, Kevin Johnson and John McNeil went to see, the dead, body.

Kevin Johnson:

It looks like, James Madison.

John McNeil:

Yes, it is.

Kevin Johnson:

What happen?

John McNeil:

No one knows, yet, but, I have my officer, investigating.

Kevin Johnson:

I'll look around too.

John McNeil:

Do that, and maybe, you, can help me out.

Take his picture along, with you.

Someone, may have seen, him.

Kevin Johnson:

Cool.

So, Kevin Johnson, put the picture, in his pocket and, called Ricky Martin, and, told Ricky Martin, to follow, him.

As soon, as they left, the other officers, were, still looking for clues.

Fade Out:

Scene II:

In this scene, Kevin Johnson and Ricky Martin, go to Club D., to find out, about James Madison.

Kevin Johnson:

I ask around, and you will do, the same Ricky.

Ricky Martin:

I will take, of it.

Kevin Johnson:

I mean, not, to hook up, with any, of these boys, in the club.

Ricky Martin:

You, act like, you know me, well.

Kevin Johnson:

I do.

Kevin Johnson and Ricky Martin, go, there separate ways, in the club.

While Kevin Johnson, was talking, to some, of the boys, in the club, while Ricky Martin, was trying, to hook up.

Kevin Johnson:

Bartender, have you seen, this man?

Bartender:

He looks familiar.

Kevin Johnson:

Tell me.

Bartender:

He use, to come late night.

He would talk to, a lot of African American, brothers.

Kevin Johnson:

Okay, so maybe, if I showed, his picture, to someone, in here, they may, know him.

Bartender:

Yeah.

So, Kevin Johnson started talking, to some of the African American, brothers.

Kevin Johnson:

Hey! Have you seen this man?

African American Brother One:

Yeah, he looks, familiar.

Kevin Johnson:

Yeah, tell me.

African American Brother One:

Well, he likes to blow, me up.

But, I would rather, blow you up.

Cause, you look good, brother.

My name is Jacob Thomas.

Kevin Johnson:

I am a cop, looking to find, and the killer, who killed him.

I am in, no need, of a blow job!

So, if you can't help me, then, get off!

Not, off on me!

Do, you hear me!

While, Kevin Johnson, was looking, for evidence, Ricky Martin, started talking to, a Latino, brother.

Ricky Martin:

Hey, what's your name?

Latino Brother:

My name, is, Jeremy Hernandez.

Ricky Martin:

Well, Jeremy, you are pretty buff, brother.

Maybe, we could go somewhere.

Jeremy Hernandez:

Yeah, we can.

So, Jeremy Hernandez, and Ricky Martin, went, to the back, of the club, where, guys can kiss, and, give each other, blow jobs.

While, Jeremy Hernandez, and Ricky Martin, was busy, Kevin went ask, another African American, brother, some questions.

Kevin Johnson:

Hey, what up?

African American Brother Two:

Hey, sexy, what up?

Kevin Johnson:

I want to know, if you know, this man, in the picture.

African American Brother Two:

Yeah, he looks, familiar.

Why?

Kevin Johnson:

He was killed.

African American Brother Two:

No man.

Are you serious?

Kevin Johnson:

Yeah.

African American Brother Two:

He gave me, a blow job.

Then, we were going, to leave, but, Butch came in.

Kevin Johnson:

Who is Butch?

African American Brother Two:

Look, over there.

He is what you call a thug, rough nick.

A brother

Like yourself.

Kevin Johnson:

I'm going, to talk to him.

African American Brother Two:

Maybe, you will stay, here with me.

My name is Anthony Simpson.

Kevin Johnson:

I am not, in the mood.

So, Kevin left, to talk to, butch.

Kevin Johnson, approached butch.

He looked, at Kevin Johnson, and went over, to see him.

Kevin Johnson:

You must be butch.

Butch:

Yeah.

But, my real name is Marcus Matthews.

Kevin Johnson:

Do, you know, this man, in the picture.

Marcus Matthews:

Yeah, I went, to a motel, and he blew me up.

He paid me, some money.

I am a gigolo.

Kevin Johnson:

He is dead.

Marcus Matthews:

I didn't, kill him.

He gave me, some money and then, I left him, in the room.

He was still alive.

But, if you want, baby, we could, go somewhere and play.

Kevin Johnson:

No

Thanks.

Then, Kevin Johnson went to find, Ricky Martin.

He saw, his partner, come out the back.

Kevin Johnson went to get him.

Kevin Johnson:

Let's go, I found, the information, I need.

Ricky Martin:

Yeah, I found, the man, of my dreams.

Kevin Johnson:

Yeah right.

Kevin Johnson, and Ricky Martin, took off.

Fade Out:

Scene III:

In this scene, Kevin Johnson drops, Ricky Martin, home and Kevin Johnson goes home.

Kevin Johnson starts pacing, in his living room and talking to himself.

Kevin Johnson:

I don't understand.

It looks like, no one, is going to, Tell me, truth.

I need more clues.

Kevin Johnson, leaves his house, and goes to, a bath house.

He gets out, of his car, with, the picture, of James Madison.

Kevin Johnson, goes into, a steam room, and wait, until, somebody comes in.

Kevin Johnson has a white, around his waist.

Then, an African, American male, comes, into the steam room.

The African American brother stares at Kevin Johnson.

Kevin Johnson:

Hey, what up?

African American Brother Three:

Hey, what up?

Want to, go somewhere, and hook up.

Kevin Johnson:

I want to know, if you know, this man, in this picture.

African American Brother Three:

He looks, familiar.

Why?, should I know him.

Kevin Johnson:

He was killed, yesterday.

African American Brother Three:

Sorry.

Was he, your man?

Kevin Johnson:

No, he wasn't.

But, I am investigating, the crime scene.

African American Brother Three:

What are you, a cop?

Kevin Johnson:

Yeah, you got a problem, with that.

African American Brother Three:

No.

I heard, cops are rough, in the bedroom.

They like to, take charge.

I think, it is a power, they have.

So, that would be, cool.

So, if you wanted to, you could spank me.

Kevin Johnson:

Brother, I am trying, to solve, this case.

African American Brother Three:

Okay, he came in.

I saw him, one night.

He likes, dark skin, brothers.

He and I, had a good time.

But, he was alive.

He left, with some, rough nick, brother.

I don't know his name.

I think, he is here, tonight.

The dark brother, likes, both dark skin, and white boys.
So, if he is here, you see a tattoo, on his arm.

It says, "Boss", on it.

On his, hard back, it is, a dragon.

On his, hard rock, six-pack, chest, he has, a tattoo, which says, "Bad Brother".

You can't miss him.

See you around.

So, Kevin Johnson waited, a little longer, and suddenly, the brother, that, the mystery brother, told him, came in, the steam room.

Kevin Johnson:

What up, brother?

African American Brother Four:

What up, brother?

Kevin Johnson:

Kevin.

African American Brother Four:

Chris.

Kevin Johnson:

Chris.

Have you seen, the man, in the picture?

Christopher Carver:

Why?

Is he your, boyfriend?

Kevin Johnson:

No.

He was killed.

Christopher Carver:

What are you, a cop?
Kevin Johnson:

Yeah.

Why?

Christopher Carver:
That is good.

I like, a bad brother.

We could dominate each other.

Kevin Johnson:

I am trying, to solve this case.

Christopher Carver:

I didn't kill him.

He and I hooked up.

But, he left, with a white boy.

The white boy, call himself, J. J.

Kevin Johnson:

Okay.

Christopher Carver:

Hey, what about, you and me, get freaky.

Kevin Johnson:

Pass.

Then Kevin Johnson left the bath house and went home.

Fade Out

Scene IV:

Kevin Johnson wakes up, and he starts, to think, of those initials.

Kevin Johnson:

J. J.

I don't know, what, they stand for.

It could stand for John Jones, James Jameson, Joey Johnson, and Jake Jones.

I don't know.

The telephone rings.

Kevin Johnson goes into, the kitchen and answers it.

Kevin Johnson:

Yeah, what up?

Ricky Martin:

Hey, brother, this is Ricky.

Kevin Johnson:

What you want?

Ricky Martin:

Where you went, last night?

Kevin Johnson:

I, went out.

Ricky Martin:

Found any boys, to play with.

Kevin Johnson:

No.

I was, trying to solve, this case.

Ricky Martin:

Not, with James Madison, again.

Kevin Johnson:

Yeah!.

Ricky Martin:

You don't have, to yell, at me.

I was, just asking, you.

Kevin Johnson:

Keep up, with what, is going on.

You are my partner, on this case.

I am tired, of you, always, trying to, have sex, with every man, you see.

Focus, on this case.

Ricky Martin:

Okay.

I will.

Kevin Johnson:

Hey

Ricky.

Ricky Martin:

Yeah.

Kevin Johnson:

You remember, a man, call J. J.

Ricky Martin:

Why?

Should I?

Kevin Johnson:

Maybe

I went, to this, bath house and talked, to a guy name Chris.

He told me James, left with a guy, called, J. J.

Ricky Martin:

I don't know.

Why, you went there, without me?

Kevin Johnson:

Ricky..., concentrates.

Ricky Martin:

Okay.

I don't know.

Kevin Johnson:

Okay, Ricky.

I will talk, to you later.

Ricky Martin;

Okay.

Talk, to you later.

Then, Kevin Johnson, hung, up the phone, and went, sit on his couch.

He started talking, to himself.

Kevin Johnson:

Those, initials, sound familiar.

It sounds like, a man I knew.

Kevin Johnson was so puzzled, he kept thinking, harder.

Since, he couldn't, figure it out.

He decided, to go, to Ricky Martin's house.

When he arrived, Ricky stepped, out of his house, and was going, to welcome, him.

Ricky Martin:

Hey, brother, get down!

Kevin Johnson:

Yeah.

As soon, as Kevin Johnson, gets down.

He went, to see Ricky Martin, who was in front, on his front door.

The two, went inside and talked.

Ricky Martin:

I don't think, I remembered, a man, with the initials, J. J.

Kevin Johnson:

Didn't, one of our friends, had those initials.

Ricky Martin:

Not, which I could, think of.

But, let me; start running, down this list.

I will tell you, the names of our friends, and you can write them down, and look at, the first letter, of the first name, and the first letter, of the last name.

Kevin Johnson:

Okay.

Get me a piece of paper.

As Ricky Martin, went find, a piece of paper, and an ink pen.

Kevin Johnson went to the couch, to lean back, and think, of those initials.

A few seconds pass, and Ricky Martin, came back, and handed, Kevin Johnson, the ink pen and piece, of paper.

Ricky Martin:

One of our, best friends, name is Gregory Hanes.

You know, he is, that dark skin, slim, brother.

Kevin Johnson:

Yeah.

The one who had a crush, on me?

Ricky Martin;

I'm sure, you remembered, Jose Miguel.

The Latino

Brother.

Kevin Johnson:

Yeah.

The buff-up thug, you like.

Ricky Martin:

Yeah.

He can freak me, all night and day, if, he wants to.

Then, there is Albert Morris.

Who is a nerd?

Kevin Johnson:

You think, just because, he is intellectual, he is a nerd.

Like a black, brother, can't be smart.

Ricky Martin:

Well, I never saw, him get laid, yet.

He might be a virgin.

Kevin Johnson:

Whatever?

Ricky Martin: Then, there is Sergio Thomas.

That Hispanic

Brother.

He is one hot tie.

Kevin Johnson:

You mean the dreamer.

Ricky Martin:

No, he is The Singer?

He has a rock hard body.

I could see myself

Kevin Johnson:

You want to discuss with Sergio and Jose, to have a threesome.

Ricky Martin:

Then, there is that, white boy.

Or should I say Caucasian, brother.

Allen Marshall.

He is okay.

For a buff up, white boy.

But, I need a black or Spanish boy.

Kevin Johnson:

Yeah.

So come on.

Ricky Martin:

You act like, you don't know, them.

Kevin Johnson:

Just remind me!

So, I can write, their names down!

Ricky Martin:

Somebody, didn't have, sex lately.

You need some, good loving.

Now, you know what.

Our friend, Daniel Simon

He is one, hot body builder, dark skin, brother.

I remember, when he won, that contest.

He won, first place, as African American Universe.

Let me tell you, he needed to win.

I wanted to get, with him.

He has the body of a god.

He has buns, of steal and he has hard rock legs.

I could wrap my legs around his.

I could press, his body, net to mind and I could press, his lips, close to me.

I could do so many things.

Kevin Johnson:

Okay.

Stop fantasizing.

Run, it down some more.

Ricky Martin:

Didn't Joey Rodman, hook up with, a guy, that had the initials, J. J.

Kevin Johnson;

Joey.

Ricky Martin:

Don't tell me, you don't remember, Joey.

He was that, dark skin, athletic, brother.

Kevin Johnson:

Joey.

Ricky Martin:

Yeah.

He ran that marathon.

It was, for Aids awareness.

Kevin Johnson;

Did, I hook up, with him.

Ricky Martin:

Yeah.

You did.

Kevin Johnson:

Why, don't I, remember?

Ricky Martin:

You were drunk.

I sure, you remembered.

Joey's after party.

You had a little, too much, to drink.

Then Joey brought you home.

You and him, well...

Let's just say.

He told me, it was the best, sex, he ever had.

I don't know, what, you and him, did.

But, he said, it was remarkable.

Kevin Johnson:

I think I did, remember.

Didn't he hook up, with, someone, who had the initials, J. J.

Ricky Martin:

Yeah.

Jerry Jones.

Kevin Johnson:

That's right.

I dated him, too.

Ricky Martin:

Yeah, he was your ex.

Kevin Johnson:

Yeah.

I know.

Ricky Martin:

Where is he?

Kevin Johnson:

When we, split up, he told me, he was going, to Hollywood.

You remember.

He called himself, Jerry Hollywood.

Ricky Martin:

Yeah, I did, remember.

Didn't he, have some friends.

Kevin Johnson:

Who?

Ricky Martin:

Linda Michelson and Tina Mc Combs.

Kevin Johnson:

I think so.

Ricky Martin:

Yeah, you know.

The Lesbians, we know?

You know them.

I call them, the fish eaters.

Kevin Johnson:

Okay, now, I remember.

Ricky Martin:

Where are, the friendly girls, at?

Kevin Johnson:

I don't know.

Ricky Martin:

Maybe, if we find them, we can find Jerry Hollywood.

Kevin Johnson:

Okay.

Let's go.

Fade Out

Scene V:

In this scene, Kevin Johnson and Ricky Martin, heads for Hollywood, California.

Both of them arrive in Hollywood.

There are going, to a club call Boys Sanctuary, at night.

Ricky Martin:

Remember, this club.

This was, the hot spot, at one time.

Kevin Johnson:

Yeah.

I met, Jerry Jones, here.

I remembered, we danced, and everyone, was watching.

Ricky Martin:

Yeah.

Because, you dance, just like him.

Just like, a white boy.

Kevin Johnson:

Whatever?

You were jealous.

Ricky Martin:

Sure, I was.

I wasn't, the fool, they were, looking at.

Kevin Johnson:

Whatever?

Let see, if Linda and Tina, are here.

As they went inside, they saw a mix crowd, of gay men and women.

Ricky Martin:

Now, I remember, this was a mix gay club.

Kevin Johnson:

Yeah, I remember.

You couldn't tell, the girls, from the boys.

Ricky Martin:

I cannot believe it.

That is why, I go to, the all American, gay boys, club.

I am a bottom, looking, to have fun.

Kevin Johnson:

Come on.

Do not, hook up.

I, repeat, do not hook up.

Ricky Martin:

Yes, mommy, I remember.

As Kevin Johnson and Ricky Martin, tries to find, Linda Michael son, and Tina Mc Combs.

All of sudden, Kevin, bumps, into Linda.

Linda Michael son:

Hey, you, watch out.

Kevin Johnson:

Sorry.

Linda Michael son:

Kevin, is that you?

Kevin Johnson:

Yeah

Linda.

Linda Michael son:

It is good, to see you.

It has been, a long time.

Kevin Johnson:

Yeah, it has.

Linda Michael son:

I'm sure, you remember Tina.

Kevin Johnson:

Yeah, I do.

How are, doing?

Tina Mc Combs:

I am fine.

How about you?

Kevin Johnson:

I'm Fine.

Tina Mc Combs:

Where is Ricky?

Kevin Johnson:

He is here, somewhere.

Tina Mc Combs:

I'm sure.

He is looking, for, his next, meal.

Kevin Johnson:

Well.

You can say that.

A few minutes later, Ricky Martin sees, Kevin Johnson, and heads, toward him.

Ricky Martin:

Well, Kevin, I found you.

Look, like you found, the dumb and scrub.

Tina Mc Combs:

Well, look, what the dog, dragged in.

Are you looking, for, your next, boy toy.

Ricky Martin:

Well, at least, I'm not looking, for, fish food.

Tina Mc Combs:

Please, boy, you couldn't handle, a woman.

Ricky Martin:

Yes, I have.

Ask, your brother, the drag queen.

I surely, gave, him a ride.

Remember, to the next block, to sell, his goods.

Tina Mc Combs:

You don't know, my brother.

Ricky Martin:

Wasn't he, on America's Next, Drop Out, and Models?

Tina Mc Combs:

My brother is a hood rat.

He has a body, of a hard rock.

If, you look up, at the booth, he is the d. j.

Ricky Martin:

That's him?

Tina Mc Combs:

Yeah.

Kevin Johnson:

Well, if you are finish, I was looking, for Jerry Jones.

Linda Michael son:

You still want to get back, with him.

Ricky Martin:

No, hooker!

He might be, involved, in a case, Kevin and I, are working on.

Linda Michael son:

What, do you mean?

Kevin Johnson:

Somebody told me, that he hooked, up with, James Madison.

Tina Mc Combs:

Not, that white boy.

He uses, to come in, here.

Kevin Johnson:

Tell me, more.

Tina Mc Combs:

I use, to see him, majority, of the time.

He always looking, for some boys, to hook up, with and everybody knew it.

I don't know him, that well.

But, he is a freak.

Kevin Johnson:

James died.

Linda Michael son:

When?

Ricky Martin:

Two nights, ago, if you knew that stupid.

Linda Michael son:

Alright, dog boy.

Kevin Johnson:

He did, die, the day, before yesterday, Ricky.

Ricky Martin:

Okay, so sue me.

Tina Mc Combs:

I think, I heard, something, on the news, lately.

Kevin Johnson:

So, have you seen, Jerry Jones?

Tina Mc Combs:
Yeah, he was, in here, yesterday.

Do you think, he is involved, in a murder case, which you are, working on?

Kevin Johnson:

I am not, sure

But, I think of, putting the pieces, together.

Linda Michael son:

I have, his number, if you need, it.

It might, work.

Just call him, if the number, is disconnect, then I will, try to find, another number, you can reach, him by.

Kevin Johnson:

Thanks, I appreciate it.

Tina Mc Combs:

Don't forget, your bitch, when you leave.

Then, Kevin Johnson went, to get Ricky Martin and then, they both left, the club.

Fade Out

Scene VI:

In this scene, Kevin Johnson and Ricky Martin are at Kevin Johnson's house.

Kevin Johnson:

I have been, trying to put, the pieces, together.

Ricky Martin:

What are you, thinking about?

Kevin Johnson:

I think that my ex has something, to do with this, case.

Ricky Martin:

You know, what you need?

Kevin Johnson:

What?

Ricky Martin:

You need, to go, to the gym, tomorrow.

Kevin Johnson:

Ricky! You are suppose, to be helping, me with, this case.

I know, all you can do, is think about, sex.

I am tired, of trying, to find one man, after another.

I want a real, relationship.

Ricky Martin:

Okay! Maybe, that is true.

But, I want to, live my life.

I have things, I want to do.

Maybe, I will go, to bed.

Kevin Johnson:

Good idea.

I can think, more.

Ricky Martin:

Goodnight.

Kevin Johnson:

Goodnight.

A few minutes, later, Kevin Johnson, starts thinking, about how, his ex, could be, mixed up, in this case.

Fade Out

Scene VII:
In this scene, Kevin Johnson and Ricky Martin, go to see Caleb Miller.

They want to talk to, the coroner.

Ricky Martin stayed, in the waiting room, while Kevin Johnson, went talk, to the coroner.

Kevin Johnson:

What can, you tell me, about James Madison's body.

Caleb Miller:

When I examined, the body, I found, that he had sex, with a male, visitor.

Because, the seaman, is still, in him, if anybody knew.

Kevin Johnson:

Okay.

Anything else, you want to know.

Caleb Miller:

Well, I notice, that, he had a stranger, colon odor.

I haven't smell, this one.

Kevin Johnson:

Okay, it smells, like J-Roc's brand.

Hard bodies, like you never, believe.

Caleb Miller:

Yeah, I wear that one.

I like J-Roc.

I think, he is wonderful, if anybody wanted to know.

Kevin Johnson:

Anything else, you want to know.

Caleb Miller:

Yeah, he ate pork-n-bean and bake chicken.

He also, had lettuce, with it.

Low-carbohydrates, if anyone guessed.

I know, it is every, gay man's meal.

Kevin Johnson:

Okay, thanks, doctor.

Caleb Miller:

Not a problem.

Hey, brother, if you want, we could go out.

I mean, you being, a chocolate, brother

I am a white, hot buff, male.

We could, get busy.

Kevin Johnson:

Not today.

Caleb Miller:

Let me know, when you want, a quick, pick, me up.

Fade Out

Scene VIII:

In this scene, Kevin Johnson and Ricky Martin, go to Ricky Martin's house.

Ricky Martin:

So, what's up?

Kevin Johnson:

I learn, that the deceased, wore, J-Roc's hard bodies, colon.

Ricky Martin:

Didn't Jerry Jones, give you that, one day, for your birthday, or did you forget, about that.

Kevin Johnson:

Yeah, but, why would, the deceased, be wearing it.

Ricky Martin:

Hello! Gay men, wear that.

It gives them, a hot body... rock hard abs... Hot lips, and an extra, long cock.

Kevin Johnson:

Ricky! Stop fantasizing.

J-Roc's colon is expensive.

Not too many stores carry it.

Ricky Martin:

So, what are, saying?
Kevin Johnson:

What if, my ex is the killer?

What if, he is trying, to hurt me?

What if, he is playing games?

I know, if wants, me dead.

I remember.

Ricky Martin:

What do you, mean?

Kevin Johnson:

Remember, when he wanted, that threesome.

I didn't.

Ricky Martin:

Okay, but, would he kill you, over that?

Kevin Johnson:

No, he was also, on drugs.

Ricky Martin:

Yeah, I remember now.

He had an angel dust.

Kevin Johnson:

Yeah, he would, hear voices.

Ricky Martin:

So, what will, we do?

Kevin Johnson:

I am going, home, to call, this number, I got from Tina.

Ricky Martin:

What number?

I bet it's your ex.

Kevin Johnson:

Don't worry, about it.

I will get, to the bottom, of this.

Ricky Martin:

I wish, you would, get to, my bottom.

Then Kevin Johnson leaves.

Fade Out

IX:

In this scene, Kevin Johnson arrives home.

He call the number, he has.

There is no answer, so then, he here a door knocks.

Kevin Johnson:

Who is it?

Man, I ask, who is it!?

There was no one there, but a note, attack to his front door.

Kevin Johnson, look at it.

It was a phone number.

He called it.

It was Jerry Jones voice.

Kevin Johnson, hung up, the phone, and proceeded to catch him.

Kevin Johnson:

I got him.

Kevin Johnson, left, his house.

Outside his car, was Linda Michael son and Tina Mc Combs?

Kevin Johnson:

What are, both of you, doing here?

Tina Mc Combs:

We are here, to help you.

Linda Michael son:

We found, Jerry Jones phone number.

Kevin Johnson:

Okay, I sure, both of you, want in, on this case.

Tina Mc Combs:

Yeah.

Linda Michael son:

So come on, let's pick up, dog boy, and roll out.

Kevin Johnson:

Where am I, suppose to be, going?

Tina Mc Combs:

You are going, to a ware house, where Jerry Jones, is at.

Linda Michael son:

But, first, freaky boy, house.

Kevin Johnson:

Get in, my truck.

Tina Mc Combs:

I can't believe this is a General Motors Corporation Truck.

Let's go

All of them went, to Ricky Martin's house.

As soon, as they arrived, at Ricky Martin's house, they had a chance to think about, what had happen?

They all get down.

Kevin Johnson:

How did, you, both know?

Linda Michael son:

We are both, government agents.

Tina Mc Combs:

We work for, the Federal Bureau of Investigation.

Kevin Johnson:
So, you both, are looking for Jerry Jones.

Tina Mc Combs:

Yes, he is smuggling drugs.

Linda Michael son:

We knew you and him were together.

We knew that he was, using drugs.

Tina Mc Combs:

We knew he was selling, Nordics.

So, he had to lie, to you and say, we knew him.

Ricky Martin comes out:

Ricky Martin:

So, what up, lesbians?

Kevin Johnson:

Don't start.

We got to find, Jerry Jones.

Get in the truck.

All of them get into the truck and leave.

Fade Out

X:

In this scene, they are fifty feet away, from the ware house, where, Jerry Jones is at.

Ricky Martin:

How did, all of you know, about this?

Kevin Johnson:

A long story, it is, so I will keep it short.

Tina, how did, you find out, all the information, that led you, up to this conclusion.

Tina Mc Combs:

I remember the dead body.

Then, I remembered, the colon.

It smells, like something, Jerry Jones, gave you.

Kevin Johnson:

Yeah, I know, that was, the mystery.

But, then, I thought, about other men, bought, that colon.

Linda Michael son:

Yeah, the world, but, when you looked, closer, you can think of yourself.

We found, a hair sample, which matches, Jerry Jones.

Kevin Johnson:

So, when, the body was in, the morgue, you both went, and did your own investigation.

Tina Mc Combs:

Yeah, we did.

Then, I notice, that, Jerry Jones, went out, one night.

I know, you were working, but I couldn't say anything.

Linda Michael son:
We notice, a man, named James Madison, was having sex, with Jerry Jones.

He was supplying Jerry, with drugs.

Kevin Johnson:
So, that is how, Jerry got his drugs.

I would have never known.

Tina Mc Combs:

Then, we follow Jerry, one night, to an old abandon where house.

We saw a man, we having been, looking for, by the Thomas Matthews.

Kevin Johnson:

That name sounds, familiar.

Linda Michael son:

Yeah, you know him.

He was the guy, which Jerry said, was his ex-lover.

Kevin Johnson:
Yeah, I remember that.

Jerry told me, he broke up, with him.

Tina Mc Combs:

He is a drug smuggler.

Ricky Martin:

Brother, how the hell, you hook up, with this bad boy.

I wanted to, hook up with, a bad boy.

I love bad boys.

They know, how to make, you feel, so good.

They can work it, in the bed, boy.

Tina Mc Combs:

We all know, freaky attic

Kevin Johnson:
Go on.

Linda Michael son:

So, as soon as we, found Thomas.

We knew he had to be, involved, with Jerry.

So, on top of that, I hope all will be well.

We had to, play like we knew Jerry.

Tina Mc Combs:

Jerry, at first, did believe us, but we suspected, that he knew, who we were.

Kevin Johnson:

Now, I know, it makes sense.

Linda Michael son:

We have to stop him.

All of them decide to head, to the ware house.

Fade Out

XI:

In this scene, Jerry Jones and Thomas Matthews are talking, in an office, which is on, the left hand side, of the ware house.

Jerry Jones:

I can't believe that we have, succeeded.

Thomas Matthews:

Yes, we did.

Now, the plan is, to leave and never, comeback.

Jerry Jones:

My thoughts, exactly, I already knew, it could come to this.

Thomas Matthews:

I thought, you and I could go, to Hawaii.

I love to spend, sometime, in the sun.

Jerry Jones:

I love, too.

Then, Thomas Matthews, decides, to get up and Jerry Jones, takes a bat, which is next to, the file cabinets.

Jerry Jones, hit Thomas Matthews, in the head and go to the file cabinet, where the money, is at.

Jerry Jones finds a duffle bag, near the desk, that Thomas Matthews was sitting in.

He rushes, to take, the money out.

After, he is finish; he is getting, ready to leave, when he sees, Kevin Johnson, through the crack, of the door.

Jerry Jones runs to the back, of the ware house.

Jerry Jones, get the bombs, to set off.

A few minutes, Kevin Johnson, Ricky Martin, Tina Mc Combs and Linda Michael son, arrives.

As they slow, creep into, the where, with their guns, in their hands.

Tina Mc Combs goes in first.

Kevin Johnson goes in next.

Then, Linda Michelson and Ricky Martin, follows behind him.

Jerry Jones, has set, the timer.

Soon, the bomb will go off, in five minutes.

Soon, Jerry Jones starts shooting.

Linda Michael son, Tina Mc Combs, Kevin Johnson and Ricky Martin, had for cover, behind an iron wall.

Linda Michael son:

Who can give yourself up, Jerry!?

Jerry Jones:

Not a chance, I am leaving, with my money and you can't stop me!

Tina Mc Combs:
You will not, get away!

Jerry Jones:

You will never get me!

Kevin Johnson;

Jerry, it's Kevin, you have, to give, yourself up!

Jerry Jones:

Sorry baby, I am leaving!

Ricky Martin:

Stop tripping!

Give up!

Jerry Jones:

Ricky, eat me out!

Cause, I am leaving this, hell hole.

Suddenly, Linda Michelson and Tina Mc Combs, started shooting.

Then Jerry Jones, start shooting.

Then suddenly, the bomb goes off.

It blows up, the office and the back part, of the ware house.

The flames, spread, to the gas tanks

Linda Michelson, Tina Mc Combs, Kevin Johnson and Ricky Martin, ran, as fast, as they can, to the front side, of the ware house.

After, the whole where house, is engulf, with flames, Kevin Johnson, sees, Jerry Jones, on the right hand side, heading out, from right hand side, of the ware house.

Then another explosion, of the ware house, occurs.

Tina Combs, Kevin Johnson, Linda Michael son and Ricky Martin, runs to Kevin Johnson's truck.

As soon, as they all get in the truck, Kevin Johnson's burns rubber.

They leave the scene.

Fade Out

XII:

In this scene, Linda Michael son and Tina Mc Combs, tell Kevin Johnson and Ricky Martin, goodbye, at Kevin Johnson's house.

Linda Michael son:

Yeah, I guess, we got, to go.

Kevin Johnson:

Yeah, sorry, we couldn't get, Jerry Jones.

Tina Mc Combs:

Don't worry, we will find him.

Ricky Martin:

I hate, to say, goodbye.

So, I hope to see, you both, soon.

Linda Michael son:

We will, keep an eye out, on both of you.

Tina Mc Combs:
Yeah, we will be around.

Then, Linda Michael son and Tina Mc Combs, head to their truck.

As they both get in.

They were saddened, by leaving.

Ricky Martin, left, Kevin Johnson's house.

Ricky Martin, get in his, Chevrolet car.

A few minutes, later, Kevin Johnson, saw, Jerry Jones, in the next door neighbor's house.

Jerry Jones waved at him.

Kevin Johnson was frightened.

Fade Out

Example of a short/short:

Christmas Time

As I decided to go shop for my family; it seems that I had notice a stranger, and it seemed that he is homeless, and all I could think of is that maybe I could help him, and I decided that since I had made enough money; even with the bonus check that I have received; it would be better to help someone, and all of sudden as I walked into the store; I started to buy two of the same gifts, because maybe the homeless had children, and a wife, and as I had bought the gifts, and as I started putting the gifts into the basket, and as I decided to check out, and as I had was headed for the counter; it seemed that I had found a young man who was waiting for customers, and as I saw him; I rushed to get into the counter, and as I started to get the gifts onto the counter, and as I knew in my heart, and in my mind that I was doing the right thing, and as I had gotten all the gifts on the counter, for the cashier to check them out, and as I had paid the young man, and as I knew that the homeless man was still outside, and as I rush to get outside, and as I seen the homeless man, and as I went towards him, and as I had said, "Hello, my name Jeremy, and what is yours?" as I had to asked him his name, and as the stranger said, "My name is John, and I have a wife, and two children; a boy, and a girl, and I need some help to help them get something for Christmas" as he had tears in his eyes, and as I said, "I have a gift for your wife, and children" as I wanted to give the gifts really bad, and as I had handle John the gifts, and as I could see the tears in his eyes, and as I started to cry as well, and all of sudden John had given me a big hug, and it seemed that it lasted for hours, and he is so happy with what I had done, until I knew he could use a job, and since my company was hiring; I wanted to help him get off his feet, and as I said, "The job that I work for is looking for new people, and I want to take you for a interview" as I really was going beyond my means, and as John said, "I really appreciate that, but I don't have any clothes" as he had his down, and as I said, "I will give you some of mine, and you can keep it" as I rushed to the car, and I has some clothes ready in the car; which I had bought, and as I rushed towards the car, and had open it, and I had open the car door, and had gotten the clothes, and had rush back to give it to him, and as I handed him the shirt, and pants, and he looked at it, and he said, "It is just my size; thanks you very much" as he was really happy with tears coming from his eyes, and as I had given him my number; I was really happy, and I said, 'Monday; I will pick you up, and you will be ready for the interview" as I knew he would be very happy, and as he said, "Thank you very much; I will tell my wife, and children" as he started to walk back to the homeless shelter, and as I went to my car, and as I had open the door, and gotten in; I knew I had did someone else a favor, and I had my own gifts for my family, and as I closed the door, and started the car, and had left the parking lot; I knew that I had done the best job ever; which is help someone else; then myself.

Example of a poem:

I AM

Who am I?

The creation that the creator has made

Hard working

I meet

Generous to greet

Serious, the Weight

Crazy, the Place

Torn from here to There

Lovers, not Fair

Anger, tamed me

Violence, wrapped me

Truth killed me

Need a better Chance

Need love, which is never there

Truth or Dare

The way is the Light

I need to believe in God's light

The creation I am

God made me to last

But a slave

I am

Example of a short play:

FAMILY CRISIS

Curtain Opens

Dialogue starts off with Jerry Jones, and Gina Waters.

Scene I:

Jerry:

I am so grateful to be a live; it seemed that Jesus let me; have another day.

Gina:

It seemed that not only you, but me as well; I am very glad as well.

Jerry:

You know what to do; I will tell you; we should go out, and invite our neighbors; who lives next door; a welcome.

Gina:

You know that seems; like the right thing to do.

As Jerry, and Gina head over to their next-door neighbors; as; Laura Jackson, and Brent Miller; is new in the neighborhood.

Close Curtain

Scene II:

Curtain Opens

In this scene; Jerry, Gina, Laura, and Brent are together; in Brent, and Laura's house.

All four characters dialog begins.

As Jerry, and Gina walks over; to their neighbor's house, and as Gina knocks; on the neighbor's front door, and as Brent; answers the front door.

Jerry:

This is a nice house; man you must have put a lot of work in the house.

My name is Jerry.

As Jerry, and Brent shake hands.

Brent:

Yeah, but man; let me tell you; I have to make sure the wife; is very happy.

My name is Brent.

Laura:

You don't have to do; tell them; the whole story.

My name is Laura.

Brent:

Baby, I want our neighbors to know; that I am putting a lot of work; in this house; for you, because I love you.

Laura:

I know; baby; I love you too.

As Gina, and Laura hug; each other

Gina:

That is so sweet; I know that my man; loves me.

My name is Gina.

Jerry:

Yeah baby; you know I do.

Gina:

I wonder sometimes.

Jerry:

Not with me; I really love you.

Gina:

It's okay; I know you do.

It is hard to find true love; in this world.

Laura:

Girl, you know it

Brent:

I think that we are the lucky ones; in this world.

Jerry:

Yeah; I think so.

As the two girls; hug, and as the two men shake hands.

Close Curtain

Scene III:

Open Curtain

Jerry, and Gina is home, and Brent, and Laura is in their house.

Jerry and Gina Speak

Jerry:

I am so glad; that we went; visit our new neighbors.

Gina:

Yeah; it seems that we are doing; our part; hopefully others will come, and join us; in inviting other people; no matter what gender, or sexual preference, or even racial background.

Jerry:

You are right.

Close Curtain

Scene IV:

Open Curtain

Brent and Laura Speak

Brent:

I am glad to meet; our new neighbors>

Laura:

Yeah; so am I

I wish people; would be like Jerry, and Gina.

Brent:

Yeah; I know what you mean.

Curtain Close

Scene V:

In this scene; Brent; walks over, and wants to hang out; with Jerry.

As Brent approach the house, and as he knocks; on the door, and Jerry answers the door.

Jerry:

Hey what's up man?

Brent:

I want to know; if you feel like talking to me.

Jerry:

Okay; I thought; that you were unpacking your things.

Brent:

Yeah; I was, but it is good to talk to; someone; other than my wife.

It seems that sometimes; a man can't tell a woman; how he really feels; since it is hard to do.

Jerry:

I know what you mean, but sometimes we have to; so that our wives know; the truth about what we are thinking, and feeling.

Brent:

Yeah; you are right.

So; what is going on; with you.

Jerry:

Well; I been working as a janitor; so it is hard work, but I am glad; that I have a job.

Brent:

Yeah; I know what you mean; some people; don't have a job.

Jerry:

That's true; so we should be thankful, or thank God, for what we have.

Brent:

Yeah man; that is something; that is hard to do.

Jerry:

Well; it is hard; to think that there is a high power.

Brent:

Yeah; since we are not familiar; with the spiritual being.

Jerry:

Should we have to think twice?

Brent:

I think; we should accept; that God exist, and leave things alone.

Jerry:

That is something we don't do; as human beings.

Brent:

I wondered; what this spiritual being; is doing?

Jerry:

Watching us; I am sure.

Brent:

Yeah, but have you ever think; that maybe he is using us.

Jerry:

What do you mean; using us?

Brent:

Well; something bad happens; to good, people; that try their best.

Jerry:

Well; I think that maybe he has to let things happen to us.

Brent:

What do you mean?
Jerry:

Well; he is bound by his words; if you read the bible.

Brent:

Does; it say that; in the bible?

Jerry:

Here is what I know; for myself.

I know that he had Ten Commandments, or laws.

Brent:

Yeah; I heard of them.

Jerry:

Well; maybe since he has rules; he has to obey his rules>

Brent:

That makes sense.

Jerry:

And so; he has to let things happen, but he does bless us.

Brent:

How does that work?

Jerry:

If we ask him; in prayer; when we pray; then; if it is in his will; then we will be blessed

Brent:

If we want something; is that what you mean?

Jerry:

It has to be something right; not something we want, but what we need; at the time we need it.

Brent:

Like?

Jerry:

Example: Well; if we need food, and we don't have the money; the angels; who are his voices; will tell us that.

Brent:

You mean God does tell us that; himself?

Jerry:

No; if he tell us something; it can kill us, because he is so powerful.

Brent:

Okay...

Jerry:

It is like this; we has humans are the creation; he is the creator.

Brent:

The rules; is something; that he lives by; just as we should live by.

Jerry:

You got it.

Brent:

That makes sense, but it is hard for us; to understand; the creator.

Jerry:

Yeah; we have to have faith.

Brent:

That is where the faith word; comes in.

Jerry:

Yeah.

Brent:

Okay; the question; is it right; that he doesn't help us; like we need him?

Jerry:

Yeah; he help us; on his time; frame.

Brent:

Alright; make sense.

Jerry:

That's it.

Brent:

Man; it was good; talking to you.

Jerry:

Yeah man; likewise.

Close Curtain

Scene VI:

Open Curtain

In this scene; Gina and Jerry talk, as they walk home.

Gina:

I am so glad; to see them.

Jerry:

I am also; glad.

Gina:

It seemed that; else could we do; is maybe; offer them; to eat; at our house.

Jerry:

Sounds like; a plan.

Close Curtain

Scene VII:

Open Curtain

As the couple; went home; as they decided to contact; the other couple; they didn't know; that; Laura had passed out.

It seemed that Brent; has to bring; his wife; to the hospital.

As Brent contacts; the nine-one-one; so it seemed that Albert Marko; answered the telephone.

As Brent dials; the operator; the operator starts talking.

Albert:

Nine-One-One

What is your emergency?

Brent:

My wife; had passed out

It seemed that I am not sure; what is going on.

Albert:

Well…

What happen?

Brent:

My wife; was washing the dishes

It seems that; all of sudden; she passed out.

Albert:

She is on; any medication?

Maybe the doctor; prescribed them; for her.

Brent:

No; not that; I am aware.

Albert:

Any stress; at home?

Maybe on the job

Brent:

She said; that she was having problems; with her boss.

Maybe; that is what is going on.

Albert:

I sent the information; to the nearest; ambulance.

Brent:

Thanks

Albert:

Someone is on their way.

I also; sent the information; to two officers; who are closer; to your area.

Brent:

Thank you; very much

Close Curtain

Scene VIII:

Open Curtain

In this scene; Isaac Walters, and Marty Amos; are the first ones; on the scene.

These are the two officers.

As they arrived; at Brent, and Laura's house; they get out of their car; then they went towards the door; they knocked; at the door.

As Brent hear the knock; he ran; to see who; is at the door.

Brent:

Yeah

Who is it?

Isaac:

I am Isaac

One of the police officers

As Brent; open the door; he tells the officers...

Brent:

Come towards the kitchen

As they all rushed; towards the kitchen; the officers seen; Laura; on the floor; as they had to contact headquarters; to let them know; that they arrived; at Brent, and Laura's house.

Marty:

WE have arrived; that the house.

It seems that we; need; assistance.

Albert:

The ambulance; is on their way.

Marty:

You will have to give us room.

It seems that the ambulance; is on its way.

As Brent; started to go; to the living room; he started to pace.

Close Curtain

Scene IX:

Open Curtain

In this scene; the ambulance arrives; John Carter, and Victor Roman; arrives.

As; the two men; had gotten out; they went toward the house, and knocked on the door.

Brent:

Who is it?

Victor:

We are the medical team.

As Brent; opens the door; he lets them in; the three men; rush; towards the kitchen.

As the two men; who are part; of the medical team; went towards Laura.

As John said; to Brent...

John:

You need to go; to the living room

We will do our best; to revive her.

As Brent went back; to the living room; he started to pace; the living room floor.

As the medical team; as they were trying their best; it seemed that they had to go; to the hospital; to see; what the doctors; can do.

As John; went to get the stretcher; it seemed that as Brent seen him; he wondered; why is going on.

As John; rushes; to get the stretcher; it seemed that Victor started to do; mouth-to-mouth recitation.

As; Victor couldn't get a pulse; it seemed that he thought; the woman was dead.

As John; came with the stretcher; it seemed that he rush; to go back; towards the kitchen.

It seemed that Brent; started worrying, and pacing; the living room; floor.

As John; open the stretcher; it seemed that as; Victor, and John; had carefully; put Laura; on the stretcher; as they knew; that they had to; rush; towards; the hospital.

As they left the house; as well as the police; was heading out.

Isaac said...

Isaac:

They are bring; your wife; to the hospital; you will have to follow; us; we are headed there.

Brent:

I am coming.

Marty:

We have some questions; to ask you.

Brent:

Yeah

As the officers had left the house; as Brent; was on his way; he had to get his keys; which are on the cabinet; as he grab his keys; he heads out; the house, and locks the door.

Curtain Close

Scene X:

In this scene; it seemed that the medical team; arrives; at the hospital; as the officers did; as well; then Brent arrives.

It seemed that as Brent arrives; he contacts; Jerry.

Brent:

Hey; it's Brent.

I am at; the hospital.

My wife collapse; on the kitchen floor

I need you come to the hospital.

My wife collapse; please bring your wife; for support.

Jerry:

Okay

As Jerry; told; Gina; what is going on; it seems; that they rushed; to get out; of the house; as they were headed towards; the front door; as Jerry; locks the door.

Close Curtain

Example of a short story:

JERRY'S WORLD
THE DARKNESS INSIDE

It seemed that; as Jerry Turner; a Caucasian male; finally escape the house; where the police; had found him; he knew that; this was the last time, or is it; as Keith Harris; who is one of the officers; on the scene; as Jerry knew him; with his distinct tattoo; since it was on his back; as the tattoo; with his name; on it.

As Keith; taken Jerry; to his car; he knew that Jerry; was scared; he was frighten; by; what happen to him; as the officer; guided in; the car; with his masculine right hand; as Keith; was an African American male; who works out; as Jerry; was thinking of.

As Keith; closed the passenger side door; which was on the; driver side; then as Keith had gotten; into the car, and close his door; with the force; of a power; which Jerry; found so; appealing

As they were headed; to the precinct; Jerry had to tell his story; as the other officers; who were: Dennis Winters, a Caucasian male; Peter Madison; a Latin male; as well as Matthew Walker; who is an African male; all these buffed up; police officers; knew that they looked real good; anyone can smell; the cologne; that these men; were wearing; the hot summer night; where their bodies; were perspiring; with so much sweat; as the officers had to brush their forehead; as they didn't find; any evidence; as Jerry was in the back; he started to reminisce; when he met Luther Patterson; an African male; he is a shape-shifter; as Jerry was unsure; who he is; since; Jerry didn't know where he was.

As Jerry; went to the bar; called: Club D.; which was really famous; for a lot of gay guys; usually; they are looking for a one night stand; the atmosphere; is really loose; as the men of so many colors, and so many body types; from the buffed up; thuggish type guys; to the guys; who wear; the most; expensive suits; to the guys; who are the regular Joes; who work; a nine-to-five jobs; while the suit wearing guys; made a lot of money.

It seems that the guys; who are police officers, bankers, to those who work; as cooks; janitors; as well; as guys who work in film, and television companies; these guys; with their tee-shirts; either jeans, or shorts; as they usually work-out; as well; as not work-out; regular guys; whose body sweat; as the other guys; can smell; the pheromones; ten feel way.

These guys; that play pool; to the guys; who gossip; like women; to the guys; who like; to be alone; well; as Jerry found himself there; while Luther; had seen him; as Jerry; looked like a scared; little boy; that he was; at that time.

With the sweats; of these guys; with the pheromones so high; these guys; who were there; want to; get with someone; that had the broad shoulders; the thick muscles; the hard rock; chest; some guys; wanted to get with the slim down guys; well; some of the other guys; wanted a little extra; meat; on their bones.

As Jerry walks in; as he decided to go; to the bar; he needed a drink; he was feeling a little lonely; Jerry was the kind of guy; that is a loner; doesn't want to hang out; with the other people; he loves to read books; especially; romantic stories.

In Jerry's mind; a good romance story; where the guys; gets his man; where he finally; gets his dues; where the cowboys work hard; live hard, and play harder; than any other guys; in the world.

As Jerry; was at the bar; Luther decided; to go see him; it seemed that Jerry; was average built; with the look; in his eyes; with the taste; of sweat; that was coming; from his forehead; since; it is a little hot; in the bar.

As Luther was there; at the bar; he orders a drink; from the hunk bartender; who is Wallace Smithson; as Wallace; is a brown skin; with a tattoo; on his arms; which says; Brotherly Love; which anyone could think of; as the bartender; with the brown goatee; as he knows; Luther's drink; which is; jack Daniels; with a shot of sprite; on the rocks; Luther loved his drink; it was hot; he was sweating; as the bartender poured his drink; while Luther; had his eyes; in Jerry's eyes.

The lust fill temptation; that Luther was feeling; as he started to; take his hands; under his shirt; rub his hairy chest; as Jerry looked at him; all jerry could think of; is his nature was rising; so hard; as Luther's nature was rising; as the bartender; poured the drink; as Luther said, "Well; you are new here" with a little smirk; on his face; as Jerry; said, "I am" as he had a smile; on his face.

The two hot; guys; with their hormones racing; as Luther said, "Well; let me show you; around" as he had a smile; on his face; as Jerry; said, "Well; I don't usually; talk; to strangers" as Jerry paused; for a few seconds; then said, "Well; since you seem friendly; I will let you; show me; around".

As the two guys decided to; take a look; in the back; as Luther had knotted his head; to his right hand side; for Jerry; to follow him; as Jerry; who wanted to kiss; Luther; which was in his head; decided; to pull back; just a little; even though; his desires is to; get with him; as Luther started to show him; the hall; where the guys usually hook-up; for the one night stands; as Luther asked Jerry, "Well; do you want to; go down the hall; into one of the rooms?" as Luther had that same grin; on his face; as Jerry said, "Well; not this time" as Jerry was holding back; so much; that he really wanted to jump; his bones.

The sexual tension; between these two guys; was so animalistic; the way they looked; at each other; the way they smiled; at one another; as Luther took his left hand, and put it; on Jerry's left shoulder.

As Luther; looked in Jerry's eyes; with a passion; that he wanted to get with him; as Luther said, "Well; we could; go to my place; if you want" as Luther was trying; all means; to get Jerry; undress.

"Well; we could; go, and talk" as Jerry said; with the notion; that they were going to get; naked; for the first time; as the two guys; walked towards the front door; of the club; the two guys; seems to be sweating; from the summer heat.

As the two men; walked out; with the hot summer night; the way they looked at each other; with the lust; in their eyes; their hearts pounding; as they walked towards; Luther's car; as Jerry was on the passenger side; as he had gotten in; then as Luther went around; since his car; was on the side; of the road; not too far; from the club; as Luther had open the door; then gotten inside.

Luther had that smile; on his face; as Jerry, and he was going to; hook-up; as Luther had put the key; into the ignition; as he was ready to go; to his house; what the two other guys; was unaware of; is that; Paul White; was outside; of the club; as he seen Luther, and the stranger; who; gotten inside; of Luther's car.

As Paul; knew all about Luther; it seemed that; as Paul recalled the events; that they were in the passion; as Paul; laid down; then Luther came closer in; opening his legs; slowly, and firm; as they two started kissing; their cocks were so hard; till the guys; knew that they had to release their cum.

As the two guys; stopped kissing, and Paul; started to suck on; Luther's peck; as Luther closed his eyes; with the hot; passionate love making; would occur; the two guys were getting; a little sweaty; since Paul; had no idea; what Luther was; so as Luther had open his eyes; he knew; that he was going to transfer; Paul; into the creature that he is; so as Luther decided to kiss Paul's neck; while had stopped sucking; on Luther's right peck; Paul close his eyes; the hot sweaty; passionate love making; commence; the two guys; were feeling each other; as Luther decided to kiss; Paul's six pack chest; as Paul; continue to close his eyes.

The hot; burning lust; continues; it seemed that the bed was hot; it almost felt as though; the room; which felt like a; steam room; as the two guys just keep grabbing; at one another; as Luther started to suck; Paul's dick; it was so hot; Paul; started to moan; just a little.

The hot night; seems so long; so hot; so fill with the night air; which was cool; Luther had the window open; as Luther had stopped blowing Paul; then Paul; had gotten up; turn Luther around; as Luther was on his back; then Paul; came towards Luther; started kissing him; once again.

The passionate kissing; turned the two guys on; the hot steamy room; with the sweat; glistening; on the two guys bodies; as they were so hot; they were unaware; of what was going to happen.

As they stopped; kissing; Paul started to kiss Luther's hard rock; six pack chest; as Luther; closed his eyes; as he was in the thresholds; of passion; this was like no other; as Paul worked his way down; to Luther's dick; as he started sucking on it; the sweat; still; slightly poured on down.

The two guys; were feeling the hot sweaty night; with the air feeling so cool; as the wind blew; as the two guys were getting a little cooler, but not much; as Paul had finished; licking the balls; then all of sudden; Luther started to get up; then he turn Paul; on his chest; as Luther started to kiss; Paul's neck.

As Paul closed his eyes; with the chance; of feeling; the love; that Luther giving him; as Luther started to slowly; go down; kissing his back; what Paul; didn't realize that; Luther had a tattoo; on his right arm; of a wolf; on his left arm; he had an image of a regular dog.

As Paul; was unaware of the tattoo of Luther's name on his back; then the picture of death; as Luther knew that; he was death; walking; as Luther continue to kiss; Paul's back; till he was getting to his ass; as Luther was an ass man; he loved to eat the cakes; of welling guys; so as he started to kiss Paul's right check.

As the two guys; started to feel; so passionately; in love; at the time; the happiness; they were feeling; was like a moment; in time; a freeze frame; of what life; could be like; as Paul; wanted to image; that he had found the man; of his dreams.

As Luther started to kiss the other side of Paul's check; as Paul; started to clutch the pillow; as he had still closed his eyes; he started to let out a moan; as Luther started to rub Paul's back; as he was getting ready; to tear him; a new whole; as Luther had it; in his mind; as Luther took his dick, and slowly; put it in Paul's ass; it was like; a moment; that Paul never wanted to end.

The passionate sexual encounter; started to make Paul; feel as though; the love of his life; was there; just for a moment; as Luther put his right arm around Paul's chest; as he started to work; Paul out.

As Luther started to let out; a moan himself; as he slowly; moved in and out; as he stopped; just for a few seconds; to kiss Paul's neck; to soften the blow; as Paul; had grabbed the pillow, and hold it tightly; the two sweaty guys; were hot, and as the wind blew; just a little more; to try to cool off; their hot sweaty; glistening; bodies; as Luther stopped kissing Paul's neck; as he continue to fuck him; slowly; as well as gently.

Luther wanted this; to be the best sex; that he had; as Luther continued to go; up, and down; as his ass; was moving; up, and down; Paul continued to moan; just a little more; then it seemed that Luther had to soften that blow; once more.

He started kissing Paul's neck; the hot passionate night; continued until; Luther had finally finished; releasing the cum; into Paul; the hot sweaty; bodies; the sticky sheet; the night blew; then after that; Luther was tired; he had to bite Paul; as he did that; at the end; of the sexual; encounter; as Paul; grabbed the pillow tightly; as he let out a moan.

Then; as the night continued; Paul gotten up; as he was feeling differently; as though; something was happening; while Luther; slowly open his left eye; he notice that Paul; was getting ready to turn into a wolf; since Luther is a shape-shifter; he could be anyone.

As Jerry; arrived at the police station; he started to notice; one of the officers; a dark skin officer; it seemed that; he act as though; he recall; the way Luther acted; which was the eye; that was on him.

The way; he had that smile; in his face; Jerry thought that; it was Luther; he was not sure; so; as Jerry was getting out; of the squad car; as Keith was helping Jerry out; it seemed that as Jerry started walking; towards the front door; of the police station; he recalled that night; where he, and Luther had made passionate love.

As Luther made it home; with Jerry; as the he stopped the car, which was a black; Chevrolet; impale; as the two of them; started to get out; as they were unaware; that Paul decided to get; his own truck; which is a Chevrolet; Sierra; classic; as Paul; had to kill Luther; who changed him.

Paul knew that his life; would be; fill with so much pain, and suffering; so as Jerry, and Luther gotten out; of Luther's car; as the both closed the door; then; as the two of them; were headed towards; the front door; as Jerry had seen the house; it is a mansion; it had blue trimming; as well; as the lawn; was freshly cut.

As Luther open the front door; as the two of them; walked inside; as Jerry looked; at the antiques; the brown chair; which looked very old; as well; as the white staircase; as he see the marble floors; Luther had that same smile; that lust fill smile; on his face.

It seemed that; in Jerry's mind; Luther was some bad boy; looking to party; looking for a good time; even a sexual encounter; that would make him; feel whole.

As Luther guided him; towards the staircase; as Jerry said, "You are such; a gentleman" as he is very impress; with Luther; then Luther said, "Sometimes; we have to be; gentleman; if we want; the person; that we mostly; desires".

As he had that grin; on his face; as the two of them went up stairs; as the passionate; would be so amazing; that Jerry would not want; to go home; it seemed that in Luther's mind; he was looking for a soul mate; this time; he had to get it right; as Luther recalls; before he was turned.

It was a night of passion; that Luther never forgotten; it was a man; name; Wesley Jackson; who was the alpha male; as they two of them met; while Luther; was looking for a good time; as Wesley drove up; in his white Chevrolet; avalanche; truck; with black trimmings.

Wesley; was is a dark skin; male; really rough; around the edges; had a goatee; he was hairy; as Luther had seen him; short brown hair; cut really fine; to the edge; as he was wearing; a white shirt; with a blue suit jacket; Luther could see his; big muscle arms; as he had on some black; slackers.

As Wesley rolled down the window; while; he pulled over; as Luther had seen him; from top; to bottom; it seemed that Wesley said, "Hey; look like your lost" as he had a smile; on his face; so Luther said, 'Well; no; I am talking a walk" as he smile back; at Wesley; so as Wesley looked into his eyes; as it seemed that they eyes locked; "At time; of night" as he Wesley knew that Luther; must be headed somewhere; to have fun; so as Wesley continues.

"Well; get in; I am going; to this club; call: Club D.; you can join me; if you wish" as Wesley chuckled a bit; while Luther did the same; as he said, "Well; why not; I suppose I will" as Luther had open the passenger side, and gotten in.

In Wesley's mind; Luther was fine; with tattoos; that he had seen; on his left hand arm; while Wesley had his own tattoos; on his left side of his neck; he had the numbers; twenty-two; eighteen; which; on his right arm; he had the name; Bentley Washington; on his left arm; he had the number; twenty-five; on his back; he had the name; Loner for life; on his chest; he had the name; bad boy of Hollywood.

A Wesley had closed the windows; as he had his air-conditioner on; as he was headed to the club; the two guys started talking, "Well; it seems that we both; are looking for a good time" as

Wesley chuckled a bit; while Luther said; as he laughed; a bit; "Yeah; looks like it" as the two of them made it to the club; Wesley parked in the back; of the club; as he stopped his truck; as the two of them had gotten out; as Wesley wanted to head towards the back; where the hall was; while; they had bedrooms; for the guys; who wanted to have; a little fun.

As Wesley taken his key, and as he open the back door; as he open the back door; as Wesley walked in, and Luther was right behind him; as they were headed inside; Wesley said, "Look; I am going to show you; what some guys do; back here.

As Wesley had open the first door; from the back; they had two brown skin brothers who are: Vin Carter, and Lorenzo Jacks; as the two guys; were on each other; kissing one another; as they were feeling the heat; of the hot room temperature.

As; Vin; who was very masculine; with big arms; a hairy chest; six pack; chest; just as Lorenzo who is very masculine; as well; big huge arms; buffed up brother; big buffed legs; as well; as Vin big legs; as well; both of them; had short hair; as Lorenzo was a little hairy; with a little bit of hair; on his chest; legs; arms, and back, but Vin; had a hairy back; as Wesley, and Luther; left that scene.

They decided to go; to the next door; as they seen a Caucasian male; with short hair; big arms, and legs; with some tattoos; on his back; which had his name; Lawrence Diesel; as he was giving; Frank Tate, a blow job; as he was sucking; in the man's dick; as Lawrence; started to feel good; as Wesley, and Luther was getting very horny.

As the white boy; started to suck; n the man's balls; as Frank; was a dark skin; brother; with a slight; brown beard; as well; as he had big legs; like some man; at a mister universe pageant; as well as big arms; he was massive; with a huge massive dick; which he enhanced; which is now; twelve inches; of huge muscles.

As Wesley closed that door, and as they went towards the next door; they seen two Caucasian males; having sex; they were average built; bears; they were; so hairy; it seemed that Aaron Marvin, and Harrison Grant.

Harrison; decided to rub; Aaron's dick; with his own; dick; Harrison closed his eyes; he moaned a little bit; as Aaron did; as well; then as Harrison; started to suck on Aaron's pecks; as Aaron; hold him tight.

As Harrison decided to kiss; Aaron's six pack chest; as softly as possible; it seemed that; as kept going down; he started to get close; enough; to suck Aaron's dick, and balls; as Aaron started to moan; then took a breath; of fresh air.

Then; Aaron; decided to grab; Harrison, and turn him over; he decided to kiss his neck; so passionately; as Aaron started kissing; Harrison's back; until he reach; his ass, as he started to kiss; each ass check; the fucking would be; so spontaneous; that they guys; would fall in love.

As Aaron; slowly push his dick; into Harrison's ass; Harrison; started to moan; with the intention; of getting off; as Aaron decided to hold; Harrison's chest; as he had to kiss his neck; to soften the blow; the next time; Aaron decides to turn Harrison's neck; slightly; to kiss him; with a passionate kiss.

As Aaron had to give him; the final touches; to make sure; that as he cum; he wanted the pleasure; to be so romantically; enchanted; like something; out of a fairy tale; where the man; gets his man; then he kiss the guy; then he suck; on the love stick; then he turns him over, and does his thing, and they both live; happy ever after.

Meanwhile; Jerry was brought to; a room; where the officer; had to question him; it seemed that Keith; was the one; who would do it.

So as Jerry, and Keith went into the room; as Keith needed to know; what happen; Jerry started to tell his story; as he started talking about the club; it seemed that Keith knows that club well.

Keith; would go there; every now-and-then; as Jerry started telling him; he met a stranger; there; as Keith started to recall; the event; when he was there; it seemed that; they had a guy name; Thomas De Nero; as he was a hunky guy; his short hair; his big arms; his broad shoulders; his big legs; then it seemed that his cock; was always hard; it could be to big; for his blue jeans; his blue shirt; his goatee; his dark skin; his big lips; as Keith started talking with him.

As the two guys; decided to go; to the room; where; they could have; the best sex; of their lives; it seemed that the guys were unaware; that a guy name Kent Clarkson, was watching them; he knew that; some unknown creatures; what people call; shape-shifters would be there; it seemed that Thomas; is a slayer.

He kills; the freaks; of nature, and not in a good way; as Thomas; been hunting Luther; as he recalled Luther, and he use to be lovers; years ago; as he was one; of the packs; years ago; as time moved on; Thomas, Luther; Wesley; Charles Kirk, Benjamin Wheeler, Larry Edison, Moses Tiberius, and Taurus Jefferson; were all in a pack.

These men; were the ones; who was suppose to take down; humanity; to make them the freaks; that the others would hate; what was told to Wesley; is that a great man; by the name of George Houston; was the creator; who had started to create; the shape-shifters; long ago;; when the world; was destroyed by the flood.

George; had survived; he started to create; a race o f shape-shifters; from the middle east; they started to collect; as many people; as to add to the cause; it seemed that the people; spread out; in secrecy; they had to hide; to fight; to survive; the food; was; whatever animal; they could catch; as time went on; as centuries were winding down; from the formation of North America; there were military officers; that are shape-shifters; as the aliens; who came to this Earth; planted the seed.

Being in slower demand; the tide turned; the modern day world; started to grow; as well; as technology; so it seemed that the shape-shifters started to grow; then Thomas; knew that he had to stop; the menace; to society; which is us; the creatures; so as Thomas knows that since; George; is dead; Wesley is still alive; he would have to gather; men; to his cause; to destroy; Wesley, and finally; break the curse.

Writing a novel; a short story; it could be short shorts; as well as novellas, even short novels; then novels; full length novels.

Companies that might be able to help you are:

New Concept Publishing

Science fiction/fantasy/fantasy romance/spicy or erotic any story length, and short stories; as well as full length stories

Spicy or paranormal romance; any length and time period

Such as: vampires, werewolves, aliens, fairies, shape shifters, dragons. Ghosts or humans with electronic sensor perception

Spicy or romance; suspense, and or ultra sexy contemporary

Romance in any length; historical romance (tighten woven unique plots)

Highly develop sexual tension with spicy or erotic love scenes in any length; time period, or place (unusual time period; welcome)

Edgy; unique plots; strong believe conflicts; between hero, and heroine; extreme sexual tension; concise story telling; combinations of dark; sexy hero; with sassy humorous from the deep

Heroine; little or subplots; 20,000-30,000 words

Marion Zimmer/Bradley Literary Works Trust

Fantasy

12 point courier; 1"-1 ½" margin; at the top and left

1"at the bottom right

1st page; name; address; phone number; social security; in the top left corner; singe; space; email; word count; title type name beneath title; leave space between name

Being of story; double space story; indent 1/2 "before story lines & page number; &last name at the top of each page; leave 4-6 blank lines & continue the story

No chapter headings; in short stories; w/sassy; humorous; heroines; interracial & characters like: east Indian; Asian; African; American/good sex w/soul mates

Carnal=chemistry between characters w/heated built up tension; love scenes that deliver; exciting emotion once they are together; vary language w/love scene/no problem w/gay strong can be subplot

Anthologies=erotic, or spicy; BDSM; anytime/setting; 20,000 -30,000 words; bondage; domination & submission; preferred; w/heroes; being dominate; partners should be romance w/BDSM as integral part; story-line along w/heavy sexual tension; captive fantasy; bondage clubs; suspense; email is:

Submissions@new-conceptspublishing.com

Send query letter 1st; also:

Tempting the beast=erotic, or spicy; shape shifter romance/any setting & period, or sub-genre; futuristic, or fantasy; 20,000-30,000 words; animals shifters; which are: wolf; lion; tiger; panther & winged men/women; centaurs; dragons; griffins & others fantasy; type of creatures hero have to be shape shifter; alpha; sexy & powerful; email with query letter

The eternal=erotic, or spicy; vampire romance; any setting & time period, or sub-genre as futuristic, or fantasy=20,000-30,000 words

Special project=legends & lore; paranormal elements; novel length is preferred & spicy

Romancing the classic=spicy, or carnal preferred, or sensual classic stories & novels like Dracula; pride & prejudice; beauty & the beast of romantic; sub-genre; suspense; futuristic; paranormal & comedy; 10,000-100,000 words

Short stories=10,000-15,000 words; for love bite series for erotic fiction; any setting, or sub-genre must include romance; elements as well as fall under the spicy, or carnal rating system;

submission; should have a letter; briefly describe; your publishing history, or writing credits & any organization; you are affiliated with; genre & story idea; a brief synopsis is 1, or 2 page; conflict & plot development; a print of manuscript; SASE; the book on disk; in rft files, or ms word; do not publishing

Non-fiction=literary works, or gay/lesbian fiction; 60,000 words; for most genre; erotic novellas; 20,000 words-39,000 words w/spicy, or carnal short stories romance; 45,000-55,000 words; no more than; 120,000 words

Jeri Smith Youness-Editor:

Looking for romantic suspense & contemporary; romance; as long as it is well research

Andrea De Pasture-Senior Editor:

Historical romance & historical erotic romance; cover letter; 1, or 2 pages

Email: andrea@newconceptspublishing.com

End of story; type THE END; send a self addresses stamp envelope-SASE

Ja Cobyte Books

Email: enquiries@jacobytebooks.com

Poetry only: 6 pones in body of the email

Invisible Cities Press

Non-fiction

Email: tia@invisiblecitiespress.com

Impreium Proviso

Novels only

Fiction/cookbook/science fiction and non-fiction

War fiction; non-fiction & children's books

3 chapters with SASE; cover letter & synopsis

Colonies=short stories-1,000-10,000 words

Speculative=3,000 words/speculative news=100-800 words

Futuristic stories:

It could be 2229

Something similar to that year

Skate Fiction

Query first; make sure to contact them

Non-fiction (articles, editorials, interviews, and humor) 300-1,500 words

Editorials= 600-700 words

Poetry=submit poems in body of email

Email: submission@skatefic.com

Non-fiction; email it at: articles@skatefic.com

Reviews non-fiction= ice-reviews@skatefic.com

Short stories=10,000 words or less

Email: submissions@skatefic.com

With synopsis included

Serial novels=10,000 words or more

1st -10 chapters with synopsis

Project length=submissions@skatefic.com

Novels/novellas=10,000 words or more; query with the first; three chapters with a synopsis=submissions@skatefic.com

Book length; non-fiction= no word limit; proposal with synopsis & 1st-3 chapters=submissions@skatefic.com

Don't forget name; age; email; short summary of writing & skating experiences; word count; status (finish, or unfinished); genre (mystery; horror, romance, and suspense)

Target audience (Children/teen or adult)

Subject line: title of book

Pupless Fiction

Book-length=romance; mysteries; suspense; action & adventure; science fiction & historical

Northland Publishing

Non-fiction; American west; southwest; Native American; art & craft & culture; regional cookery; western lifestyle & history; interior design; architecture & gardening

Double space; seen SASE

Rising Moon

Pictured books; Spanish/English stories; southwest flavor stories &southwestern twist on traditional fairy tales

Activity books-coloring books; maze books; fun books about the region/boardwalks

The Book Den

100 pages

100,000; or 70,000 or 80,000 words

Query letter

Title of manuscript

Genre

Target audience

Add age range

Estimate number of words

Brief synopsis-single paragraph

Agree to contract

1 line description-30 words

Author's biography written in 3rd person

Under the name of author

FIC 00000-book store/category

Fiction/general

Convincing sale pitch

Sample of the best part

Name of work for sample/ chapters

Author picture

Chapman Publishing

Joy Hendry

4 Broughton Place

Edinburgh, Scotland

U. K.

E H 1 3RX

44-135-557-2207

Email: info@presspress.com.au

Four way

Only in March to submit

Four Season Publication

Novels=50,000-150,000 words

Non-fiction=complete manuscript

Poetry & short stories= enough to make a book

Children's book=complete manuscript

New World Publishing

P.O. Box 660

Randallstown, MD 21133

1-410-948-8088

Trimaxxpublishers.com

Trimaxxpublishers@yahoo.com

Javon64@trimaxxpublishers.com

Book companies looking for manuscripts:

Email them:

submissions@3rdmose.com

stompncr@aol.com

poetry@420pus.com

submissions@63channels.com

quandaries@yahoo.com

tarpoetry@blacklawrencepress.com

albaeditor@yahoo.com

cinquains@hotmail.com

manchesterboy90@hotmial.com

nov3rdsubmission@yahoo.com

rtf-5 poems

cordite_submmsio.doc

Name; short bio & contact info-submission@cordic.org.au

Fiction submission

wr.submissions@gmail.com

Flash fiction= 1,000 word

Stories= 5,000 words

Except of novels= 50,000 words; brief synopsis of novel

General overview

poetry@wordriot.org

Non-fiction=1,000-5,000 words

Short non-fiction= 500 words

non-fiction@wordriot.org

Big Bridge:

walterblue@bigblue.org

Big Bridge Press

Around September

Poetry, fiction, non-fiction, essay, journalism &art

Manifest Press

Manifestpress@yahoo.com

Attention: Michael Cross

Department of English

State University of New York at Buffalo

306 Clemens Hall

Buffalo, NY 14260

15 pages; the most

Oct.-Jan/Apr.-July

Lynne Rienner Publishers

1800 30th St.

Ste. 314

Boulder, CO 80301

1-303-444-6684

Fax: 1-303-444-0824

Proposal:

1. Book title
2. Info on author
3. Summary
4. Adults
5. 3,500 words/ 22 pages
6. Complete manuscript

Poetry

The Bitter Leander Press

4983 Tall Oaks Drive

Fayetteville, NY 13066-9776

Poetry

Short stories=2,500 words

Wings-press.com

Whitewolf.com

Willowgate.com

Ye old font shoppe

P.O. Box 34

Vernon, CT 06066

Poetry only

Walker & Co

435 Hudson St.

New York, NY 10014

1. Please write brief summary=2-5 pages
2. Please send a brief outline of each story
3. Please send 2 sample chapters
4. Please send your bio/resume as attachments

Total word count: 65,000-75,000 words

Submissions-zonemag@gamil.com

5 poems only-zafusy@gmail.com

yuanyang@hkusua.hku.hk

3-5 pomes/short stories-5,000 words

With this company; who have to send

In the body of the email; send:

A cover letter page with author's name; address; contact information; email &list of works published-send work as attachment

3 poems

urhere@arizon.edu

yawp@uottawa.ca

Brochure

publisher@wordsonthestreet.com

8,000 words for:

editor@summersetreview.org

Here is the rest of the information of slush:

100,000-130,000 words; they also take fantasy novels

Name; email; address & phone number; on cover page & 1st page manuscript; other email addresses; if anyone have one; make sure that novel is in rtf; format; style of fonts= C G omega & lucida bright time roman or courier

1 ½" margin; on all four sides

Science fiction only:

slush@baen.com

15-18 pages; business books

Author name; summary; this is an e-book company; don't forget the title; & number of pages; if more than 15-18:

submissions@bizarrebooks.com

submission@cyberageadventures.com

Science fiction; humor; romance; fiction; political commentary & poetry; masculine oriented

Times roman 12 fonts; 1 page summary; cover letter; brief biography of author; if you have been published; name; address & phone number; as well as word count.

info@cybermanbooks.com

With this company; any genre:

submissions@stonegarden.net

Twight times:

Fiction from 1,000-10,000 words

Essays: 3,000 words

Poems=30 lines

publisher@twighttimes.com

Stone dragon press

Science fiction; fantasy & horror

Email: submission guide lines

Stone dragon style sheets

Email: stonedragon@stonedragonpress.com

Sirius Publication

Short stories-5,000-50,000 words

Science fiction & fantasy; non-fiction (How to/self help/reference books)

Fiction (romance)

Query will be done on website

Scorpoius Digital Publishing

Science fiction; fantasy & horror

submission@scorpiusdigital.com

Silver Lake Publishing

Query: name; address; title of book; genre & word count

40,000 words

Science fiction; fantasy & horror; mystery; thriller; historical & romance

Salvo Press

Mystery; suspense; espionage & thriller novels

Santa Monica Press

How to books

Rowan Press Inc.

Fiction; fantasy (pagan); short stories; poems & line art; how to books

Short stories; poems; all must be in doc format, or rtf format

12 times

1-2 sentences bio

Line art-jpg images; 300 dpi format

Email: jrbrowans@yahoo.com

Regent Books

Short stories-any genre; 6,000 words

1,000-6,000 words

Poems-60 lines

Email: voyagemag@zyworld.com

Zumaya Publications

Fiction/non-fiction-65,000 words

Children books-35,000 words; which have to be lessons

Erotica can be part of the plot; right hand corner

Name; address; phone number; email; word count &genre

1'' margin; single space; new roman times; 12 fonts

Word perfect, or rtf files; when it comes to children books; it can be 35,000 words

Fiction-50 pages, or 5 chapters; non-fiction-summary; as well as table of content & summary/synopsis

Gloria@tatnuck.com

Buying guide department: 1-800-869-0366

Mystery Love's Company=1-800-538-0042

Kathy@mysterylovesco.com

Terry=1-619-258-4905 extension: 110

preed@lafourch.org

Winter wolf publishing:

Fiction=60,000 words

Non-fiction=experiences in writing; non-fiction

Short story compilation=40,000 words

Poetry; send query to:

queries@winterwolfpublishing.com

Synopsis & 1st chapters; send attachments in Microsoft word file

1" margin all around; indent 1st line of each paragraph

Except the 1st line of each chapter/new scene

Separate each scene by putting asterisks in the center of the line; format header to show; last name & title in the upper left hand corner & the page no#; in the upper right; top left cover page have: name; address; phone number & email; place approximate word count; on the top of the cover page.

Hohm Press:

hpedit@cableone.net

Send queries; religious studies; spirituality; parenting; relationship; natural/alter native health/biography/memoirs & the blues music

Ibbetson St. Press;

3-5 poems/cover letter w/SASE

Winder River Press:

submissions@windriverpress.com

Send query letter; send poems; send to Alice; usually except in October.

Disk Us:

Subject: disk us-book submission/attachment

In .htlm/.doc or .rtf files

Query letter; brief description of manuscript; non-fiction; brief synopsis of story; fiction; genre; your writing background; address &email

submissions@diskuspublishing.com

Also send short fiction; non-fiction; short stories & novellas

1,500-15,000 words

Marilyn@diskuspublishing.com

Included in subject box: disk us quick press or disk us confessions; when send a query letter; include word length; genre & brief summary w/email; double space; 12 font; times new roman w/paragraph; indented; page number; can be included; top of manuscript; name; address; city; state & zip; phone

12 blank lines; title of manuscript; ©/copyright by: year manuscript is written; 2 blank lines; body of manuscript; chapter title; 1 blank line; page break at end of chapter; 8 lines; next title; 1 blank line; 2 blank lines; the end; page break if: footnotes included; author notes; as well included, or add ending; 8 blank lines; foot notes & other add ending/beginning

Black Death Books

P. O. Box 588

Effort, PA 18330

Query/cover letter=name; address; email & past publishing credits; a brief 1-3 page synopsis; 1-3 chapters & SASE

Genre=horror; sci-fi & dark fantasy

Word counts=70,000-100,000

Also other publishing companies which are:

Demonic Clown Press:

Pulp; nior; weird & humorous; b-style horror

Word count: 25,000-50,000

As well as:

Necrolily Books:

Horror; paranormal; erotica & romance

Word count: 70,000-100,000

Romance & erotica; straight; gay lesbian; bi; underground; weird; experimental & BDSM (bondage; disciple; dominance; submission; sadism; masochism)

Blackest Death Anthologies:

Genre short stories=vampires; ghosts; ghouls; were-animals; magick; Wicca; haunting; Goth; angst; experimental & erotica

Stories that stretch boundaries of imagination; poignant stories or stories that are well plotted & generate uneasiness in the reader; death can be a factor; 10,000 words; in rtf files, or doc files; attachment; in subject box put: the blackest death; single space; time new roman; 12 point; (1") inch-wide margins all around with (w/) name; page number (No#); title of work; one on every page; on title page; into email; overview of the gist; of your story; writing credits & contrasting information send to;

blackestdeath@khpindustries.com

Double Dragon Publishing Inc.

Sci-fi novels with alien themes

submissions@double-dragon-ebooks.com

Arial/ time roman; 12 point font; double space; in rtf files; contact info; short synopsis; author's bio & photo; describe the book; 2-3 paragraph; 5-6 paragraph blurb

Dragon Tooth E-Books:

Fantasy (heroic; mythic; sword & sorcery; urban contemporary; magical & dark fantasy)

Magic plays a pivotal role/key factor; character interesting & plot reaches logical conclusions; arial or times' 12 points; double space; number justify margins; name & title is on the 1st page; in upper left hand side of each page & page no# on the right hand side; done in header part; of the document; 35,000-150,000 words; in rtf files & send manuscript as attachment to:

Lazette.gifford@double-dragon-ebooks.com

Subject line: submission & title of book; in the email; a short blurb; 250 words; give a taste of the story; think blurb as TV guide review

Dragon's Heart Romance:

Historical=set during past-era; do your research

Contemporary= set during this generation & reflect current cultural mores-suspense novels; may qualify; maybe more sexual

Inspirational=set during any era & containing spiritual; themes & attitudes

Paranormal=set in this world or another world includes-horror; fantasy or sci-fi

Young Adult=characterized by 1st love; type relationship; 1.1-2; no sexual contact; send to:

romance@double-dragon-ebooks.com

Zumaya Publication:

Science fiction; fantasy; thriller; horror; mystery; historical fiction; non-fiction; western; historical romance; children/juvenile; Christmas/seasonal; mainstream fiction romance; gothic; young adult romance; historical fantasy & true crime

65,000 word count preferred; children & young adults-lesson/moral in story; children books have to be 35, 000 words; non-fiction-for wide audience

Erotica=erotic must be part of the plot; development of character; top right corner of title page; name; address; 1' margin; no headers, or footers; phone numbers; fax number (if the person have one); email; word count & genre

No widows; orphans; single space; time new roman; 12 point; no spacing; between paragraph; rtf files; or word perfect; attachment

Non-fiction; if people are use; get a release; form or get them to sign a form; synopsis; table of content & 5 chapter

Fiction= brief synopsis & 5 chapters, or 50 pages; send to:

acquisitions@zumayapublications.com

New Concept Publishing:

Query letter/ submissions@newconceptpublishing.com

Book length; don't for get to double space

Full length novels=90,000 words & up/360 pages & up

Midnovels=61,000-89,000 words/244-356 pages

Category=40,000-60,000 words/160-240 pages

Novella=20,000-39,000 words/80-156 pages

Sensuality Rating:

Sweet=behind closed doors; sex/very mild love scenes & sexual encounters

Sensual=love scenes; comparative to most romance novels

Spicy=heavy sexual tension; graphic details & more sexual encounters

Caral=graphic sex & language; may be offensive; to delicate readers; contain many sexual encounters & include unconventional sex; not found in romance novels; may/may not be romance; typically known as erotica; historical romance; fantasy romance; contemporary romance; romantic suspense; futuristic/science fiction romance

Paranormal=ghosts; fairies; psychics; fire starters; superheroes; skin walkers; mystery unexplained phenomenon

Has to be: somewhere exotic; introduce elements of the forbidden/taboo; domination/submission voyeurism; fetishes

Historical romance=darker; torment/flawed characters; emotionally drenched; gothic or epic adventures

Futuristic romance= add change world; new galaxies; nanotechnology

Fantasy romance=dragons; manticore; centaur; unicorns; add interesting creature & magical abilities; one picture (pic) adventure or deal with social issues; such as: racism/overpopulation; men have to be: romantic; cultured; strong; capable; take charge & witty; no nerds/wimps; hero should demean the heroine or humiliate her or vice-versa

Elements= edgy; unique; plots; strong believable conflict; heavy sexual tension; concise storytelling; combination of dark; sexy heroes

Scrybe Press

Short fiction in horror; fantasy, or science fiction/novels

editor@scrybepress.com

For new authors; submit; name; story title; genre; word count& brief synopsis w/subject line: intent to submit & story title w/document attachment; in doc files, or rtf files; send story in separate email

Staple-bound chapbooks=5,000-20,000 words; $50 pays; plus 10% on the gross sales; free fiction=0.01 per word up to $25; trade paperback=$200 in advance; plus 10%; on gross sales- word count=25,000 or up; short fiction=less than 2,000 words; is also accepted.

Mundania Press

Novels; 40,000-100,000 words; sci-fi; fantasy; horror; mystery (detective &thriller) romance (no erotica); histories; western & mainstream; in doc files, or rtf files; in time roman; you can use;

underline; dashes & dots; ½ " on the 1st line; of each paragraph; use an asterisk; on scene, or point of view breaks; cover letter; in subject line add: Submission-title; title of book; your name; email; genre; word count & address; in body of email.

Synopsis=present tense; when you add it

Book blurb=summary for back of your book; send to:

submissions@mundania.com

Immanion Press

Fiction; innovative & intelligent; novels: dark fiction; literary fantasy; sci-fi & horror; slip stream/magical reality fiction & black comedies; don't want; derivative/tween high character driven; in sci-fi & visceral gore horror

Non-fiction=thought provoking; well research & boundary crossing; non-fiction work; on magic; kabala; tarot & associated thematic; in subject line: word count; in pdf files, or plain text; 50,000-120,000 words; double space; 12 points; new time roman; w/1" margin; all around & pages should be numbered; 2-5 page synopsis of book; chapter break down; for non-fiction; 30 pages; to be sent; also biographical; information of the author.

Include any published work; indicate; if manuscript is finished, or not; how many drafts; send to:

editorial@immanionpress.com.wox.org

Bohemian Ink Publishing

Novels only; fantasy; science fiction & literary fiction; send to:

submissions@bohemian-ink.com

Give a brief introduction; of your novel & your writing history; as well as query letter; which will include: name; address & phone number & email

synopsis=3 pages or less; chapter 1-3; 12 font; time new roman & double space; page no#; book title & author's name on every page

Analog Science Fiction & Fact

Double space; indent paragraphs, but no extra space; between them; author's name & address; on 1st page; pays 0.06-0.08 for short stories; which can be 7,000 words

7,500-10,000 words; will pay $450-$600

0.05-0.06 for longer than 10,000 words

2,000-7,000 words; for short stories

10,000-20,000 words for novelettes

40,000-80,000 words; for serials; fact articles which pay 0.06 per words

Sarabande

10 poems; can be added; first send query letter; w/ SASE

Pearls Street Publishing

Email; query letter about work; make sure the work is complete; summary; is required; poetry; is accepted; no# of words; biographical notes about author; which is 50 words, or less; 250 words, or less; is required for manuscript, and email:

thepearlteam@aol.com

Magazine Publisher:

editorial@yogafish.com

albisher.dan@yahoo.com

portellia@sympatico.ca

Novels:

info@epressonline.com

Essays:

philomathysubmission@yahoo.com

mindalteringcreations.com

Travel Magazine:

Word count: 400-500 words=$40

500-700 words=$55

750-1,000=$75

1,000-1,250 words=$100

1,250-1,500 words=$140

1,500-2,000 words=$155

scott@terramagazine.net

overmydeadbody.com

1st query; mysteries only

Non-fiction=mystery related author interviews/profiles & articles; mystery related travel pieces; have to be over 500 words

Fiction=taut absorbing; original work; keep dialog & narrative consistence w/characterization'; unless you use discrepancy; as a plot; word count is: 750-4,000 words

Photos=model releases & subject identification required

Ellora's Cave

Erotic romance

Full story synopsis/1st chapters & final chapter; by email; at attachment; in doc files, or rtf files

Email: submissions@ellorascave.com

50,000 words, or more; contain sexual content & language that is explicit & leaves nothing to the imagination; not romance; erotica; send to:

mckenna@ellorsacave.com

Mainstream; if not erotica; send to:

submissions@ellorascave.com

No: pedophilia; rape as titillation; bodily functions; necrophilia; knives; & stabbing weapons; stuffed in various parts of the female anatomy & bestiality

Genres:

Capture/bondage; contemporary; fantasy; futuristic/sci-fi; historical; paranormal romance suspense; time travel (past); vampire/werewolf & western

Themes:

Fables & fairy tales; gay & lesbian; holiday; interracial; ménage a trios, or more; rubenesque; and shape-shifters

Cicada Magazine:

Short stories; poems & 1st person essays; written for teens & young adults

Fiction=realistic; contemporary; historical adventure; humor; satire; fantasy; science fiction; (main protagonist should be fourteen years, or older)

Also a genuine teen sensibility; story should be for high school, or college students

Non-fiction= 1st person; experience for teens

Poetry=serious, or humorous; rhymed, or free style

Other=book review provided in depth thoughtful commentary

Fiction=up to 5,000 words

Novellas=up to15, 000 words

Poems=up to 25 lines

Book review=300-500 words

Down State Story

Short fiction, or narrative written to the standard of fiction; under 2,000 words; shorter is better; send SASE

Painted Bride Quarterly

Send 5 poems

Irish Page

Only poems

Sasquatch Books

Non-fictions only

Attention: The Editors

119 S. Main

Ste. 400

Seattle, WA 98104

Salvo Press

P. O. Box 7396

Beaverton, OR 97007

Send a SASE; as well as a query letter; this publisher takes:

Mystery; suspense; espionage, and thriller novels

Banda Press

Only short novels; which is:

12,000-20,000 words

Type: courier/new courier

Double space & left justify only

Upper right hand corner; with name; address; phone number; 3rd of the down center; book title; center your name; on new line; last name; title of book & page no#; don't start each chapter; start w/a tab button; one sentence; between each word; one space after each sentence; as well as SASE.

With these two companies; make sure to send:

A short bio & prior publication

In body of email:

Poetry-dsr@webdelsol.com

Fiction:

submissions@webdelsol.com

Star Image Publication:

Only take submissions in September

Queries first; with name; address; title; genre & word count; as well as summary; make sure you send query in the body of the email; fiction/stories publisher@silverlakepublishing.com

Daw Books:

Sci-fi & fantasy

Entire manuscript w/cover letter; double space w/1'' margin; all around; no# your pages; consecutively & title of novel; on each page; name address; & phone no#; in the upper right hand corner; of the 1st page; under that put length of manuscript; in the number of words; make sure your mail; manuscript

Edge:

Sci-fi & fantasy

75,000-100,000 words; add; depth & insight; believable behavior; motives & relationship; solid science; magic system; life form (alien); & environment; SASE; email; send query letter 1st; as the introduction; of the author; next in the letter; put why the author wants to be published; add writing history; add name; address; phone number & email; synopsis (summary); number of words; name; address & telephone number & email address; title of story; a novel by: author name.

Make sure; left space lines down from the top; left two spaces; down from previous line; centered 16 space lines; down from previous line, and send 3 chapters; chapter number form; of chapter x; centered; 8 space lines; down from top of pages; only on the 1st page; text of the chapter; justify, or left; 4 spaces down; from previous line

Books Unbound:

Fiction/Non-fiction/Sci-fi/Fantasy

300,000 words

1 page; query letter; genre; audience; synopsis; 1st-3 chapters & short paragraph of character description & author's bio

Non-fiction=bibliography; make sure to research; which can be about cities, or any non-fiction stories; make sure that you include the source material & qualifications; experts; in the non-fiction stories; as well as author's bio

Send submission:

Submissions2booksunbound.com

Make sure; it is in rtf files; when you send attachment; explain it in a few sentences;

Blind Side:

Novellas/novels

Novellas=20,000-44,000 words; synopsis & 3 chapters

Novels=45,000 words

Period pieces; foreign settings; subtly supernatural; lush atmosphere & character-driven (not plot driven)

No: children protagonist; futuristic, or depending upon technology; small evil town; non-human characters; such as: vampires; werewolves; zombies; elves; fairies; aliens; cthulhu); high fantasy; science fiction; humor; detective cop crime mysteries; writers as protagonist; over use of angels and/or demons; gore for gore sake & sex for sex sake; make sure; it is in doc files, or rtf files; attachments

Blindside@blindside.net

Send: cover letter w/synopsis; publishing credits & contact information; make sure you send query 1st; also publish at:

Pocket side: dark literary; poetry & art

Wicked Hollow:

Dark literature; poetry & potential cover illustration; dark fiction; horror; dark fantasy; general fiction; gothic short stories; 2,000 -4,500 words; poetry with gothic flair; can be 5-6 poems; phone no# & bio; double space stories; fiction; make sure; add word count; to:

wickedhollow@blindside.net

Fiction submission; in subject box; poetry; submission in the subject box

Brudage Publishing:

Poetry mail it to:

Franklin B. Ressegue

Room 203

Executive office building

33 W. State St.

Binghamton, NY 13901

1-607-723-9535

1-800-723-6008

Fax: 1-607-723-9536

Dandelion Books LLC

5250 S. Hardy Dr.

Ste. 3067

Tempe, AZ 85283

1-800-861-7899

Fax: 1-450-452-1580

Short stories; must be=65,000-70,000 words; as well as novels

Book Den:

Poetry

Send query letter

Submission@thebookden.com

Cedar Hill Publishing:

P.O Box 905

Snow Flakes, AZ 85937

1-928-536-5217

Atlantic Bridge:

Fiction; paranormal; fantasy; romance; horror; science fiction; adventure; mystery; western; historical non-fiction and poetry

Send to:

linda@atlanticbridge.net

Send the 1st; 3 chapters; in rtf files

Send:

Cover letter; address; phone no#; email; fax no#; short overview of story; genre & word count; bio & synopsis

Rex Dale Publishing Co.

Send query 1st; to:

P.O. Box 563

Hackensack, NJ 07602-0563

Poetry=100 pages ½ themes

Non-fiction=children books about mental & physical challenges; cook book & occult themes

Send query 1st, or outline; synopsis & sample chapters

Fiction= mystery & suspense thrillers; query 1st or outline; synopsis; & sample chapters

RLN Online:

Non-fiction/fiction

Send a description; of your work for review

RLN & Co.

P.O. Box 61219

Seattle, WA 98141

1-206-362-5685

Fax: 1-206-830-9091

submissions@rlnonline.com

For Poetry send to:

editors@forpoetry.com

Send 2 poems; with cover letter; brief bio; with poem

Electronic Press:

Fiction-novels & short stories collection

No sci-fi or fantasy

Non-fiction=politics; current events; history; ecology; popular science & essays; 1st query; email submissions to:

submission@electronpress.com

Attachment separate files; 2-3 chapters; which can be 25-30 pages; word perfect; Microsoft; or rtf files

Eepie Press:

Novels-fiction-spy & crime

Send submissions in Microsoft; to:

submissions@eepiepress.com

Carinfex Press:

Attachments in word, or email

Fantasy; horror & science fiction; non-fiction; children's fantasy; send information such as: bio; make sure word count is: 20,000 words; if it is children's fantasy is can be 12,000-20,000 words; anyone can send; epic fantasy; swords & sorcery tales; horror; which must be scary

No: vampire; zombies, or serial killers; the children stories; for 4-8 years old; for non-fiction; a proposal 1st; word count; & plot; bio; 1st-3 chapters & synopsis

Browzer Book:

Query on website

Baen:

Science fiction & fantasy

Science fiction add: solid scientific & philosophy

Fantasy=magic rigorously coherent & integral

Send to:

slush@baen.com

Make sure you send it in: rft files; also send; name; address; phone number; send all in cover letter & 1st page & plot outline

Awe-Struck:

Heat wave romance; short stories; novellas & novels

Contemporary; historical; science fiction & fantasy

Storm surge=sensual sizzling & stimulating; exclusive couples; married, or unmarried

Imajinn Books:

Romance/urban guidelines novels

Supernatural; paranormal; fantasy & futuristic romance: ghost; psychic & psychic phenomena; witches; vampires; werewolves; shape-shifters & futuristic in space; add atmosphere; hero/heroine must be: vampire; werewolves; etc; dark overtone; straight romance must be focus of the story; hero led character; in 3rd person preferred; 1st person will be considered; heroine must be a strong woman; always a match for hero; the hero-bold & brash; end is happy story; 70,000-90,000 words; query 1st

Erotica guidelines=1 man/1 woman; both heroic make a commitment; contemporary; historical; paranormal; futuristic & fantasy; lots of sex; parts of the plot; has to sexual charge; circumstances from 30,000 words; novellas can be 15,000-30,000 words

Holiday House:

Children's book publisher; fiction; non-fiction & picture books; query 1st; SASE; SAS postcard; middle grade novels; 32 pages & 144 pages

Four Walls Eight Windows:

124-800 pages; novel; non-fiction; history; politics; short stories; science fiction; current issues; science; religion & world rights-outline, or sample chapters w/SASE

Faber & Faber:

Poetry only

Internationally reply coupons

The Florida Villager Magazine:

Fiction/non-fiction pieces; poems=4-5 poems; 30 lines; vignettes; narratives; personal experiences & fiction; 1,000 words; suspense stories of Halloween; Christmas; Chanukah; notepad; email: csvillager@aol.com

Imperium:

Non-fiction; sci-fi; fiction & children books; send the 1st; 3 chapters

Invisible:

Non-fiction novels

Children book publishers:

1. Harcourt
2. Hall Inc.
3. Frederick Warner
4. Farrar
5. Candle Wick
6. Carol Hoda
7. John Wiley
8. Jewish Lights
9. Hyperion
10. Holt
11. Just Us
12. King Fisher
13. Lerner
14. Lothrop
15. Mill Brook
16. Morrow
17. Orchard
18. Parachute
19. Peach Tree
20. Pfeifer
21. Pleasant
22. Prolingue
23. Royal

24. NBM
25. Silber
26. RVS
27. Stemmer
28. Tricycle

Four poems; make sure you put your doc files; make sure you send as attachment

sub@journeybookspublishing.com

Book of Dark Wisdom-horror

Back Brain Recluse-science fiction

Apex Digest=weird; thriller; spatter punk; science fiction; horror; hard science & dark fiction

Aoife's Kiss:

Poetry/sci-fi; short stories; fantasy; science fiction; horror; sword & sorcery

aoife@samsdotpublishing.com

Wind River books

Fiction/non-fiction/poetry/anthologies & collections

If under 40 pages; it will be a chapbook

submissions@windriver.com

Send query letter

Writer's Exchange Publishing

Action/adventure; Christian (fiction/non-fiction); fantasy; general fiction; historical; humor; mystery; parenting; poetry; romance (straight w/paranormal; mythological creatures; time travel); looking for vampires & werewolves; self-help (health; advice & hobbies); western writing advice

Send it to somebody & that you are in closing; a book; for evaluation; genre; word count & pages; blank lines; between paragraphs; no indent marks; put exclusive rights, or distribution; make sure the file is in doc files; rtf files, or text in email; send to Mrs. Sandy Cummins at:

submissions@writers-exchange.com

Waltsan Publishing:

50,000 words; non-fiction; fiction; science fiction; how to; romance; children's stories; cookbook; collection of poetry & short stories

Universal Publisher:

Non-fiction novels only; autobiographies

The Tor Books:

Science fiction/fantasy novels

1st-3 chapters; w/synopsis; cover letter; genre & if published; double space; use 1 side of page; large fonts to read it; no margin justification & proportional spacing; rag right margin; draw wavy lines; boldface; beneath the affected characters; cover letter; also add: title; genre and date of submissions

Adrion dack review=Oct. 15

The American drive: funny material

Story fiction; 3,500 words; poems; up 2-6 poems

editors@anderbo.com

Astro poetica=Nov. 1- June 30

Personal Poems:

theaurorarerewiew@gmail.com

2-5 Poems; fiction; 300-500 words; non-fiction; 300-500 words; in the body of email:

editor@banyanreview.com

10,000 poems project; national Steinbeck center; one main street; Salinas, CA 93901

Name; address; phone; email & title

Fax: 1-831-796-3828

Oxford University Press U. S.A

Does biographies

Queer Poems

Gibosonma@ucmail.com

jamma@fuse.net

Post Road Magazine:

Need word documents

submissions@poindexteronline.com

Poetry Bay:

P.O. Box 114 North Port, NY11768

poetrybay@aol.com

S. Poetry Super Highway

La Petite Zine

Level

Lowe Press & Poetics

New Yorker

Nidus

Notell Motel-Oct. 06

Deadline: Sept. 06

poetworks@aol.com

Rattle

The Real Eight View

Sein Undwerden

Subtle Tea:

5 poems

dounsinger@subtletea.com

Tertulia

Tripych Haiku

Vox

Wild goose Poetry Review

Manic D Press:

Jan & July

Buy one book & read before publishing; manuscript submissions

Poems=5-10 poems

Short Stories=3-5

Novels=send summary & 1st chapter

Fantasy; sci-fi & fiction:

Sci-fi; poems; short stories; 65killobites; large files

Text only in email

Nightwares.com

nwpressquery@nightwares.com

Firstbook.org

1319 F St.

NW

Ste. 1000

Washington, DC 20004-1153

1-202-393-1222

Fax: 1-202-628-1258

Ideal Publications Inc.

Guide Post Magazine:

Inspire story

750-1,500 words=$250-$500

250-749=$100-$249

249 & under=$25-$99

The Editor

Guide Posts

16 E. 34th St.

New York, NY 10016

Inner Circle Publishing:

522 Sadie St.

Ste. 2

Laurens, IL 50554

1-712-841-2844

Spiritual works; w/overview; 1st chapters book; poem=7-15 & overview of book

Italica Press

595 Main St.

Ste. 605

New York, NY 10044

Author Bio; summary; 1st-3 chapters

readawhile@optusnet.com.au

Obadiah Press:

April 22

Publishnow@moderoom.com

Fiction/non-fiction; poetry; children's readers; milkweed editions

1011 Washington Ave. S.

Open Book

Ste. 300

Minneapolis; MN 55415

Poems=60 pages

Cover letter; manuscript & SASE

Submissions:

Max It Publishing Inc.

P.O Box 700

Lompoc, CA 93436

Historical fiction; sci-fi; inspiration; religious manuscripts; SAS post card

Cover letter=1 page tell us about; your book & why you wrote that story; tell what the story is about; how it is similar to other works; how is your story good for Max It Publishing

Synopsis=10 pages; lay out story in chronological format; characters in uppercase letters; only in synopsis

Mac Adam/Cage Publishing:

1555 Sansome St.

Ste. 550

San Francisco, CA 94104

Cover letter w/brief synopsis; author bio & 30 page sample w/ SASE

Romance; sci-fi; fantasy; supernatural; self-help; poetry; thrillers; religion; spirituality; children's & young adult; cookbook & parenting; family military; science & medical

Proposed book title; table of content, or 12 page summary; info about the author; target audience; estimated length of the entire work in characters; words, or double spaced manuscript; pages (pg./pgs.); include a sample pg. & expected manuscript complete; what date & indicate what material can be review

Luath Press Ltd.

543/2 Castle Hill

The royal mile

Edinburgh

EH1 2ND

United Kingdom

Manuscript; synopsis & sample chapters; a short bio of author; a prepaid envelope; for return & anything else of relevance

Leaping Dog Press:

P.O. Box 3316

San Jose, CA 95156-3316

Attention (Attn.) Editorial

Phone/fax: 1-877-570-6873

A cover letter; for publishing w/L. D. P. & Marketing title; a proposed table of content; a bio & list of publishers; 2 chapters, or 20 pages; fiction; 6-poems; no more than 12 poems

Do not publish:

Mystery; sci-fi; self-help; romance & dog books

328 Flatbush Ave.

Ste. 240

Brooklyn, NY 11238

1-212-726-1293

Fiction=3 chapters; no more than 40 pages

Non-fiction=send query letter & synopsis

Poetry=20 pages no more than 5 poems; per page & SASE

Mattell Inc.

Chapbooks

190 Parkway

W.

Duncan, SC 29334

1-617-761-3000

Send to a lady Susan; novels only; fiction/non-fiction; send a 50 page synopsis; also query letter, and bio of author

Send Query:

Jeanne@thewildflowerspress.com

Paste Poems; in email; 6 poems:

journal@solopublications.com

Editorial department:

Soft Skull Press

55 Washington St.

Ste. 804

Brooklyn, NY 11201

Attention: Poetry

10 pages

Poetry:

skinticketspublishing@hotmail.com

Bio as a poet

Shoelace Publishing Inc.

Make sure it is 10 poems

P.O. Box 530849

Henderson, NV 89053-0849

3 poems w/bio & outline:

Sheree@iol.ie

Editorial Assistant:

Synopsis & outline; author resume; 2-3 chapters; double space in upper & lower case letters& SASE

Shambhala Publication

300 Massachusetts Ave.

Boston, MA 02115

Send query:

Sovereign@thesanitypatrol.com

Six Gallery Press

Centre for the study of theory & criticism

John Labatt visual arts centre 20 of

The University of Western Ontario

London, Ontario

W6A 5B7

As if they accept poetry:

Sagabooks@shaw.ca

If they accept poetry:

rothetek@rothetechnologies.com

Ronsadale Press

3350 W. 21th Ave.

Vancouver, B C

V6S 1G7

Canada

1-604-738-4688

Fax: 1-604-731-4548

Fiction/non-fiction:

submissions@rlnonline.com

Public House Press:

Fiction/non-fiction

P.O. Box 640409

San Francisco, CA 94164

Attention: Literary Contest

SAE

Magazine

Maurice Riordan:

6 Daniels Rd.

London, U.K.

SE15 3LR

Poesy Press-Submit only in February

Scholarship &criticism:

Poetry/fiction

Gothic12@aol.com

Gothic Press

C/O Gary William Crawford

1701 Lobdell Ave.

No. 32

Baton Rouge, LA 70806

Make sure that the fiction is: 20,000 words

Sword & Sorcery:

flashingswordsae@yahoo.comco.uk

Poetry:

panicpoetry@which.net

Orchises Press:

Query first

P.O Box 20602

Alexander, VA 22320-1602

Ocean Publishing

P.O Box 1080

Flagler Beach, FL 32136-1080

publisher@oceanpublishing.com

Send query letter

Henry Morrison:

Novels; women fiction; mystery & science fiction; fiction/non-fiction; word count; summary of book; short stories are: 1,500-99,000 words

Novels=100,000-900,000 words

Pitch-Black LLC

Mail manuscripts
3232 S. 1st St.

Springfield, IL 62703

1-217-529-8089

Fax: 1-217-529-9246

picth@pitchblackbooks.com

Poems

Book Pearl:

6300 Power Ferry Rd.

Ste. 600/272

Atlanta, GA 30339

Fax: 1-419-828-8202

Author's bio; short & long term goals; as well

Book-em@bookpearl.com

Jerry Entertainment Agency/New Generation Publishing (Book Publisher)/J-Man Publishing (Magazine):

Handles screenplays, and literary works; such as: novels; collection of short stories/novella/poetry

274 Highland Rd.

Ville Platte, LA 70586

Or

123 Gobert Rd.

Ville Platte, LA 70586

BET Books

Black Entertainment Books

Arabesque Romance

Heroes & heroines

85,000-100,000 words

300-400 pages

Romance plot & interaction; between couples

Mystery; adventure, or humor

Man=issues of trust; tall dark & handsome; fears some others flaws; not dishonest

Woman=beautiful; smart & successful; fears; not a man haters; no emotional, or sensual relation; with no others

Cover letter with previously published work; 2 or 3 page synopsis; covers plot; first 3 chapters; name & address on 1st page; typed & double spaced with 1 inch margin

Sepia Imprints:

90,000-100,000 words, or 300 pages; contemporary & historical novels; suspense-driven thrillers; mystery/adventure; explore strong bonds; of sisterhood & relationship issues & offer realistic display of life

New Spirit:

Well crafted & features strong characters; overcome challenges & obstacles; the power of prayer & faith; tragedy & triumph; empower; motivate; empower & strong; non-fiction; should be 70,000-89,000 words; make sure; to send a cover letter; explain the story & previously published works; 2 or 3 chapters; name & address must be on the 1st page; typed & double spaced with 1 inch margin

C/o Karen Thomas

Editorial director

Arabesque/Bet Books

850 Third Ave.

New York, NY 10022

Glenda Howard

Bet Books

850 Third Ave.

16th Floor

New York, NY 10022

Attention: Fiction Editor

Or Feature Editor

P. O. Box 1778

Auburn, WA 98071-1778

Pearl 1

Poetry=2-5/10 pages; same poem

Fiction=1,200-4,000 words with cover letter &SASE; September-May; except material; at these months

3030 E. Second St.

Long Beach, CA 90803

Between 60-80 pages/4 poems

California Agents:

1. Peter Fleming Agency
2. Independent Publishers Services
3. The Angela Rinald/Literary Agency
4. Spieler Agency/West
5. Waterside Productions Inc.

Art Time Poetry

Send SASE

editior@ttatomag.com

New American Writing

369 Molino Ave.

Mill Valley, CA 94941

Poem-5 of them

Poems Only

offtherocks@gmail.com

Off the rocks-submission

Voice Net

P.O. Box 936

Powell, OH 43065

1-740-881-6182

Everypoet.com

New York Agencies:

1. Susan Zeckendorf
2. Writers House
3. Witherspoon
4. Wieser & Wieser
5. The Sheppard
6. Russell & Volkening
7. Helen Rees
8. Aaron Priest
9. Perking Assistant
10. The Literary Agency
11. James Levine
12. Ellen Levine
13. IMG
14. Hult House
15. Farber
16. Ethan
17. Connie
18. Sheree
19. Patricia
20. Aardvark

CHAPTER FIVE:

Gwenfontenot@theacadian.com

Which is advertising sales?

If anyone needs a grant to get books published; call:

1-800-518-4726

Ninja Gold Fish:

DVD Productions

1-213-842-1566

Fax: 1-603-699-8450

Disc Makers

7905 N. Crescent Blvd.

Pennsauken, NJ 08110-9810

1-866-270-9507

Lyrics to Jeremiah Semien Christmas Time Holiday 3:

Chorus:

We are going on a trip

Since Christmas time is here

All we have to do

Is see the children

Playing in the snow

Laughing away

As they fall in the snow

Verse One:

Driving down in a blue Chevrolet truck

Going to meet others

Cary on the madness

That some do

So all of us can do

All we want to do

(Chorus)

Verse Two:

As the cold wind blow

As we see the Christmas lights

As we keep going to

Grandmother's house

Grandfather is waiting

At the front door

Freezing cause he knows we are going

Ready to meet and greet

Every one in the house

Bridge:

We are going on a trip

Going to a family event

Since Christmas time is here

We are ready to have a great time

All we have to do

Is do what we do

See the children playing

As the ice keep falling down

Laughing away

Winter time is here

As they fall in the snow

So we do

Verse Three:

As we arrive

The fire is burning

As we get down

We see the family

Running in the house

Kissing our families

On the cheek

As we come in

Winter is the best time

Of the year

(Chorus)

Lyrics to Jeremiah Semien Christmas Time Holiday 4:

Chorus:

Christmas is here

Sleigh bells ringing in my ears

Come get up and wipe away all the tears

Verse One:

Let me in

So I can go buck wild

The girls call me

So I'm in town

Fast to get a suite for

A special occasion

Body is worn out

For shopping at the mall

(Chorus)

Verse Two:

Ready to pick flowers and candy

Got a lot of loving

Too share with you

Say my name

In the heat of passion

Fire burning as we lay down

(Chorus)

Bridge:

Christmas time is here

We can stay together

Sleigh bells ringing

In my ears

So we can cuddle

Up for Christmas

Come get p and wipe away

All the tears

And never get up

We can stay together

All night

That is what's up

Verse Three:

As I do my thing

Out of door

Got a lot to spread

Cheer for all

Party time is here

We can go

Time to go

When we have enough

Wild parties are all

In the works

So come out

We call all

Get buck wild

(Chorus)

www.ingramcontent.com/pod-product-compliance
Lightning Source LLC
Chambersburg PA
CBHW051314170526
45166CB00002B/539